D1562076

Other Books by Cherise Kelley

Dog Aliens 1: Raffle's Name (2012)
Dog Aliens 2: Oreo (2013)
Dog Aliens 3: She Wolf Neya (2014)

High School Substitute Teacher's Guide (2012)

How I Got Him to Marry Me: 50 True Stories (2013)

My Dog Understands English!

50 dogs obey commands they weren't taught

Cherise Kelley

ISBN: 1494263807
ISBN-13: 978-1494263805

Cover Design by Annette Tremblay

www.midnightwhimsydesigns.com

DEDICATION

To all of our dogs.
We love you, and we know you love us.

CONTENTS

ACKNOWLEDGMENTS

Thank you, everyone who contributed a story.
I am so happy to have "met" all of your dogs!
With joy, I introduce them all to the world.

INTRODUCTION

By Cherise Kelley

I got the idea for this book from our Queensland Heeler / German Shepherd mix dog, Raffle. For the funny story of why we named him that, read my novel, *Dog Aliens 1: Raffle's Name.*

Raffle loves to eat grass and then spit it up in the living room. Gross, huh. Also, when we adopted him from the animal shelter, they told us to give him lots of jobs and keep him busy. They said he was such a smart dog that if we didn't keep him busy, then he would find things to do, and that we wouldn't like what he found to do.

One of Raffle's jobs is to keep the kitchen floor cleaned of food spills. He's very good at it, and he also scrapes the dishes for me before I put them in the dishwasher.

One night after we had cleaned up slobbery grass off the living-room carpet, I was making dinner. Some canned green beans spilled onto the kitchen floor, and Raffle walked right by them. He wasn't doing his job of keeping the kitchen floor cleaned of food spills. Still a bit exasperated at him for making a mess in the living room, I said to Raffle,

"Oh, so you'll eat grass, but you won't eat green beans, eh?"

Of course I wasn't expecting a response, but I just about fainted when Raffle came over and gobbled up the green beans! He understood what I said!

Instinctively, I knew Raffle couldn't be the only dog who ever acted on something his human said but had never taught him. That's when I got the idea to post a paid assignment on a writing site and pay people for their true stories about things their dogs did in response to what they said just once and hadn't taught their dogs.

There are fifty great stories in this book. Some of the dogs saved lives. Some just did silly things. Some are really funny stories. Others are just cute. All of them demonstrate how dogs are man's best friend. I hope you enjoy all the stories and share them with your family and friends.

I pop into the middle of some of the stories with my notes, and then I'll see you at the end of the book, in my conclusion about dog communication research.

I don't know for sure that all these stories are true, but I don't think I paid enough to make it worthwhile to make anything up. Truth is easier than fiction.

This first story is especially amazing. Enjoy!

1 CHLOE THE GOLDEN BEAGLE

*I whispered, too scared to speak in my
normal tone. "I need Dad, Girl."*

Nobody really knows how Chloe arrived. One day, I was going through the back porch to go out to the yard and found her curled up in a laundry basket, asleep. She was only eight weeks old at the time. None of the neighbors were missing a puppy, and after a search to find the owners, we decided to keep the golden Beagle. Little did we know that we were adopting a puppy with extraordinary wit and intelligence.

At first, she was your normal dog. She learned multiple tricks in three languages, but we didn't think that was out of the ordinary. She became loved by the entire neighborhood, as well as our close friends and family. Anytime we had a visitor, they wanted to see Chloe. The kids would ask her to knuckle-bump with them. The little ones liked holding out their hand and saying, "All for one!" waiting for her to place her paw on the back of their hand to signify, "And one for all!" from The Three Musketeers. And of course everyone wanted to see her dance to Michael Jackson and do the doggy moon walk. Chloe loved the attention and soaked it up.

One day, Chloe's role in the family changed.

It all began in the wee hours of the morning in July. Everyone in the house was asleep. My older sisters were in the master bedroom that they shared. My dad was down the hall from my room. As for me, I was curled up with Chloe on my bed.

The hours rolled by, and while normally the sun would have come up, it didn't that day. The entire sky was covered in clouds, and the wind had started to pick up. Before long, the sirens were on, warning the city of a storm. The sirens woke everyone up except for me.

By the time my eyes fluttered open, Hurricane Elvis was already underway.

The entire house was shaking by the time I woke up. The wind angrily pounded at the window with such force that I was sure it was going to break. I sat up and tried to flip the light on, but the power was out. Terrified, I climbed off the bed and hid between it and the wall. I was still disoriented from just waking up, but I remember vividly not being able to hear anything except the storm. As I sat there though, I heard a noise from outside the room.

Mustering up the courage to pull myself up on my knees, I opened the door just in time to see the living room window shatter as a tree flew through it.

As I watched the storm raging inside the house, I grew worried for my sisters. I called for them, but they didn't answer. I could feel the panic swelling up inside me, taking over. I looked over my shoulder. Chloe was close behind me, and I told her to stay. Then, I began my journey across the living room. The plan was to crawl underneath the tree. I could reach the bedroom that way. As I crossed the living room, the wind pushed up.

Before I knew it, the entertainment center was on top of me, pinning my legs down.

Try as I might, I couldn't move. I now realized the predicament I was in. Thankfully, Chloe hadn't listened when I gave her the command to stay. As soon as I was trapped, Chloe was on her stomach, crawling to me. I looked at her with tears in my eyes, and with a whimper, she nudged me.

I whispered, too scared to speak in my normal tone. "I need Dad, Girl."

That was all I said. I never expected anything to come of it. After all, I had never taught her a command that was anywhere close to this. I was only telling her because it made me feel more comfortable. I was so scared, and hugging and talking to my animal made me feel better. But before I could pull her into my arms, she pulled herself out of my grip and ran back in the direction we had come from.

I closed my eyes, trying to ignore the cold that pressed against my unprotected body. I was rapidly growing numb. I could hear Chloe barking, but faintly so. I didn't realize what she was doing. My dog was getting my dad's attention. Within seconds, he was alerted to the situation and was fighting the storm to get to me. It didn't take much for him to get the window blocked off and the entertainment center off of me. The rest of the storm was waited out quietly.

That was how Chloe became so much more than just the family pet. She saved my life, and all because she understood English so much more than we expected her to. Chloe is amazing, and I will never let her go to another family. I will never stop being thankful to her. It's been ten years now, but I remember vividly the bravery my dog showed.

[Cherise's note: Don't you love this story? I do! It's an example of a dog being disobedient, yet loyal. The dog disobeyed the command to stay, but showed loyalty by following her human and then getting help for her. Sometimes dogs are smarter than humans.]

2 BOBBY THE COCKERPOO

*I need you in those bushes, digging up
whatever you can.*

Bobby, or "Bobdog" as we sometimes affectionately called him, was with us for fourteen years. He showed up at our door one random summer day when I had just finished sixth grade. He acted not only as if he owned the place, but as if he had always lived there. He sat patiently on the deck and enjoyed the sunshine until we brought a bowl of milk and some crackers (all that we had at the time, since we didn't have any pets in the house), and once he'd gobbled them up, he upgraded to phase two of operation ingratiation: making his way into the house.

Bobby's winsome demeanor and coat of curly black-and-white fur won us over after only a day of intense debate about whether we should try to take him to the shelter or find an owner. We researched dog books exhaustively in an effort to pin down exactly what breed of dog we were dealing with, and we stuck him with 'Cockerpoo' because there wasn't another breed in any of the books we'd skimmed that looked anything like him.

The Cockerpoo is known to be one of the most intelligent dog breeds, and if we had any doubts that Bobby was one of them, they were erased when he made it clear just what an exceptional brain he had on him.

I've always talked to my pets as if they could understand me. From my parakeets to my hamsters to my fish to my turtles, I've debated, ranted, lectured, and waxed lyrical. I never expected any animal to comprehend these things, but of course, until Bobby came to us, my animals were primarily those with a rudimentary to mediocre intellect.

Bobby had always watched me attentively while I was in the garage, organizing my natural history collection.

Over the years, I amassed quite the display of skulls, fossils, birds' nests, butterflies, shells, and feathers, and whenever a new addition was made, Bobby appointed himself chief inspector, and examined the object, with twitching nose and arched eyebrows, to ensure its suitability. I came to see Bobby as an assistant in these museum studies, and 'recorded' my impressions of my findings while he was in the vicinity.

I was examining my skull collection one day and lamenting the loss of an important specimen, my squirrel skull. I had found a complete squirrel skull a few years back, with the two massive yellow incisors intact and a complete set of teeth to boot. The little skull had fallen to the garage floor and been partially crushed by the car. I held up the damaged skull and complained to Bobby:

"I don't like having imperfect skulls in my collection. We really need to go on a walk and see if we can replace this thing. I need you in those bushes, digging up whatever you can."

Bob's tail wagged and his tongue lolled in acquiescence. As soon as I stepped into the cornfield, Bob lurched ahead of me, panting and scanning the freshly plowed soil. Our walk started as many did, with Bob racing to this and that spot and pausing to turn his head towards me and make sure I was following him. Bob was usually so overjoyed at being allowed to go on a leashless walk through the cornfield that he didn't think much about tracking all the mice, voles, shrews, and rats that he was bred to find. I noticed something, though, as we got farther into this particular walk: Bob's head was lowering and his pace was beginning to slow. His movement lost the calculated randomness of over-excited Bobby and seemed to be guided by an invisible force that wished to drag him through a series of arcs and ovals weaving in and out of the brush line at the edge of the cornfield.

Bobby's curly-haired figure darted in and out of the brushes, nose still planted firmly at soil level and stubby tail moving back and forth in a slow, agitated twitch. I called to him a few times because I had wanted to move on a linear path, but he either didn't hear me or was choosing to ignore me. After craning my neck for ten minutes trying to keep my eyes on Bobby, I saw him vanish deep into the brushes.

I crashed clumsily through the tall grass, periodically pelted with grasshoppers and crickets but still detecting faint vibrations far ahead of me that I assumed were the motions of Bobby. The grass only got taller, and traveling through it became more and more arduous until I gave up altogether and sat on a rock, resolving to wait for Bobby's inevitable return. I watched a pair of cardinals squabbling in a dead tree nearby and listened for any rustlings in the grass, but heard nothing. Within a few minutes, I was beginning to doze off.

I was awakened by the sound of Bobby plopping himself down beside me. He was panting and covered in burs. I asked him what he'd been up to and he didn't respond. Once I'd gotten to my feet, Bobby followed suit, and that's when I saw the prize he'd brought me.

It was a woodchuck skull. The dog had almost read my mind, because it wasn't necessarily a squirrel that I had to have. I would have been happy with any rodent, if only to possess the spectacular yellow incisors of a well-preserved skull. I will never know how clearly Bobby understood my words, but at some level, he knew what I needed for my collection and knew how to use his instincts and built-in skills to get it.

[Cherise's note: This one is incredible! There is no explanation for it other than the dog understood what his human said. The words she said that I guess the dog knew were 'walk' and 'digging'. Perhaps her body language while looking at the skull communicated to the dog what she wanted.]

3 ELLIE THE COONHOUND

*Then, hoping her blood legacy could
somehow be our salvation, I regrettably
shouted two small words, "Get it!"*

We call her Ellie, a two-year-old black and tan Coonhound we adopted only a few months ago. She has a persistent but loving way about her, very gentle as dogs go. Nothing seems to get to her or affect her fifty pound, houndish mannerism. As soon as I set my eyes on her, I knew she was the one I was looking for! She'd lived in the animal shelter for a few months. I could see her stress and she'd sustained a drawn out appearance. Nevertheless, I could see right through all of that. I could see the real Ellie behind that ruse of nervousness and disparity.

Then there is Delilah, my wife's purse-pooch kind of dog, all eight pounds of her! They call her a Chiffon, a cross between a Bison Griffin and a Shih-Tzu. I usually do not admit it but she is a cute little dog and I am quite fond of her. She is robust and energetic; I do believe she thinks she is as big as Ellie for she struts around the house and yard with the authority of a Great Dane!

After about a month, we also noticed Ellie becoming gentler with the little half-pint of an animal that is Delilah. In fact, as the two played Ellie would lower herself to the floor to 'level the playing field,' so to speak. There are times I am afraid that Ellie hurts Delilah, but she knows she did wrong and tries anything she can do to get back into "good graces" with her. Sometimes the big Coonhound forgets that she is indeed a large animal!

The four of us live in a pastoral farming countryside sharing our little slice of heaven with many other creatures that you would normally find in the Northern Michigan woods and forests.

Often we take the two dogs out for excursions through the fields and woods for exercise and for the simple reason that we all like the adventure. One thing we noticed is that Delilah will never let Ellie out of her sight, even if she has to jump straight up in the tall grass to find her! Those two have made a bond since Ellie's arrival, and now where Ellie goes you can be sure Delilah is not too far away.

There was an instance when Delilah became confused, and it was not a very good time to become confused, for any of us.

It was looking overcast that day, the clouds moving ominously across the sky, but we still decided to go out for a walk one afternoon. We really did not wish to cancel our daily excursion, despite a few sprinkles.

Crossing a large hay field, we headed toward a

wooded area with the wind against us. I did notice Ellie acting strangely but that was normal when heading into unexplored countryside. Reaching close proximity to the edge of the trees, Elli's nose bounced from the ground and up into the air, which she had done oftentimes. This time was different. I knew it myself but was uncertain how to respond to my intuition.

Delilah ran straight to the edge of the tree line, as she would normally do to catch up with Ellie. She stopped, frozen in her tracks. I heard a grunting sound and a prominent exhale from a large beast coming from a large patch of blackberries and underbrush. Ellie heard this too but did not know what to do with this new information.

Then the animal stepped out from the undergrowth of bushes and blackberries. It was a black bear no farther than five feet away from Delilah, scared frozen in place as if planted at that spot.

From the corner of my eye, I saw Ellie, her gaze concentrated upon the bear, the hair on her back and neck standing straight up, only making brief glances towards me.

I was not ignorant of what my Coonhound was capable of, and one of the animals Coonhounds hunt and track … is the bear. I also knew that when you hunted with Coonhounds you used a pack of them, but I only had one! It was apparent she did not know what to do, at least to me.

Delilah was in serious danger because the black bear, usually on the docile side, apparently felt threatened and was becoming more irritated by the second. Surely, Delilah was a goner! And the rest of us were in danger, too, for that matter.

The bear raised itself a little and came down, stomping its feet on the ground, obviously a warning sign shortening the distance. And then it raised its paw. It appeared that the bear's paw was raised to swat poor little Delilah!

I glanced back at Ellie. She struck a look back at me. Then, hoping her blood legacy could somehow be our salvation, I regrettably shouted two small words, "Get it!"

Without hesitation, as if those words were what she longed to hear, she bolted out toward the bear in four long strides. As soon as she reached the side of the bear, she let out with a short houndish bray and quickly jumped back, dodging toward the back of the bear at a relatively safe distance, braying and barking from behind.

The bear spun and attacked Ellie, but the seemingly aloof hound now had the endurance and agility of a deer! Ellie sprang back and continued to carry on.

I knew people hunted with hounds in packs and that Ellie was following that strategy. I found anything I could to throw at the bear while shouting. The bear turned back to me but Ellie closed in, nipping at the back paws of the bear until it turned back around.

Delilah retreated to the arms of my wife while she coaxed her to come and drew back across the field.

Ellie played nip and tuck while I kept with distracting the bear until it withdrew, with Ellie giving chase. I searched for Ellie until I found her. Except for slight bleeding from the end of her ear, she was perfectly healthy!

4 COCOA, OUR CHOCOLATE LAB/BEAGLE

I commented, "I just wish we could find some treasure."

When we moved to Florida last year, I knew it was the right decision for our family. We quickly began to enjoy all that our section of Florida has to offer, from its beautiful beaches to the historical landmarks. Our family, however, did not feel complete. Something was missing. We all wanted a puppy. It just so happened that our friends' dog had puppies in September. We agreed to take one of them. So, in December, we drove four hours away to pick up Cocoa, a 10-week-old chocolate lab/beagle mix. She was adorable and learned commands like 'sit' and 'lie down' with ease. Within the first two weeks, she was house trained.

We enjoyed taking Cocoa with us when we went to the beach or to friends' houses. Everybody fell in love with her. She was so soft and full of energy.

Before we adopted Cocoa, our family had purchased a metal detector. With all the historical events that had taken place in this part of the country, we figured we could find some wonderful treasure. Folks with metal detectors and headphones can be seen with great regularity on Florida's beaches. One woman we met told us each time she went out she found at least 50 cents but sometimes close to three dollars. She had found gold rings and Civil War relics.

This was going to be our ticket to untold riches.

The first few times we used our metal detector we found bottle caps, iron bars, and aluminum foil—not the kind of stuff one can make their fortune from. One afternoon we went to the beach as a family, Cocoa included. After the kids and I used the detector and spent time digging, we returned to our chairs and the rest of our family.

As I sat in the chair I commented, "I just wish we could find some treasure."

No sooner did I finish my sentence than Cocoa stood up and started digging in the sand. It was flying out from between her back legs. My son tried to make her stop, but she growled at him. Nobody was going to get between Cocoa and her hole.

After five minutes of digging and flinging sand all over everything, she had a hole that was one foot deep and one foot wide. She paused, turned her head toward us, and started whining. We got up from our chairs and walked over to the hole she had dug. There, on the bottom, was a quarter. The salt and sand had formed a crust over it, but it was definitely a quarter.

This was Cocoa's first treasure.

We praised her and gave her a treat. Once we got home, we put Cocoa's quarter in a jar. We wondered if this would be the only treasure she'd find or the first of many.

The next weekend we went back to the beach, Cocoa and metal detector in tow. My husband set up our canopy, and we unfolded the chairs and placed them underneath, out of the sun. I picked up the metal detector, hoping to find something more significant than a quarter. As I traced the detector along the sand, it made a beeping noise. My kids picked up their shovels and began to dig. The farther down we dug the more the detector beeped, but we were unable to find any object. Frustrated, we stopped digging.

My oldest son said jokingly, "Maybe Cocoa could dig again and find it."

Cocoa barked and started digging.

Since the hole we had dug was already quite deep, Cocoa's whole body was quickly out of sight from all but those who stood behind and were pelted by the sand as it flew out of the hole. She stopped digging, backed out of the hole, and whined. I reached in and pulled out a round piece of metal that was so crusted over I could not tell what it was. "Great job, Cocoa," my son said sarcastically. Laughter ensued. We each patted Cocoa on the head, and I gave her a treat since she did find the item that registered on the metal detector.

After returning home and putting all the beach items away, I retrieved a hammer and small pick from one of my son's excavation kits. I took the crusted-over piece of metal and began to pick away at it. It seemed that for all my effort only a few grains of sand were flaking away at a time. This object must have been in the sand for quite some time. I had the kids each take a turn. It was my daughter who was able to chip the largest section away. Underneath the crust was what appeared to be an Indian headdress. It was somewhat faded, but we could make out the feathers. We soaked the metal in lemon juice and any kind of acid we could think of, but nothing worked. We chipped at it a while longer but were not able to make a dent in the years of debris that had caked itself to this object.

When we found the time a few days later, we took it to a local pawnshop to see if they could shed any light on this treasure. The man we spoke with said he thought it looked like an old Civil War coin, but he could not be sure because it was too crusted over. He offered us five dollars. Since we did not want to waste any more time picking at sand and the coin was of no use to us in that condition, we took the money. We stopped on the way home and used the money to buy Cocoa a toy.

So, even though we did not make a fortune from Cocoa's dig, she was able to find what we were after, and who knows? Maybe she will unearth something of real value in the future.

5 GUS, A CAIRN TERRIER

I used the spade to plant the Scarlet Plumes.

Gus' full name is Augustus McCrae Flowers of Oz. The name Augustus McCrae came from the character of a famous western novel titled "Lonesome Dove." Flowers is our family name, and Oz was his mother's name.

Gus is a big dog trapped in a little dog's body. The four-year-old, brown-bodied, black-snouted Cairn Terrier, fully grown at 14 pounds, was the runt of his litter but is vivacious as ever. His liveliness compliments his extraordinary range of vocals that he loves to use to get anyone and everyone's attention. When one of his toys falls into the pool in the backyard he immediately trots into the living room, sees who's there, goes back outside, sits down near the edge of the pool, and yaps. His yapping, however, gets customized for whoever he found inside the living room. If it is my father he discovered, it is a low-pitched, single bark. If he finds me, it is slightly higher. If he finds my sister, his yap is much higher, and for my mother, even higher.

After we realized what he was doing with these custom yaps they were cute at first. That is until we realized that he was kind of manipulating us. We understood it as a hierarchy of yaps - a low yap for the alpha male of the house, a slightly higher one for the omega, and so on until it reached my mother. It is very interesting that a completely domesticated animal had developed this range of vocals to communicate to what he must have considered his pack, my family.

My aunt had been living with us for a few months, and she moved in with her grey terrier named Scout, who was also male and twice the age of Gus. He had picked up all of Gus' behaviors—including barking at the pool cleaner and chasing squirrels and lizards—except for his vocal talent.

One relatively cool summer evening, most of us were sitting outside on the back porch sipping sweet tea, munching on pretzels, and talking loudly to be heard over the cicadas. My parents love to work in the backyard and have made it into quite the sanctuary.

My mother was telling us about some recent gardening she had done near one of our three water fountains and was talking about how the spade she had used broke that day and cut her finger. During her story, she got tongue-tied several times on trying to say,

"I used the spade to plant the Scarlet Plumes."

We all laughed at how silly it was to get tongue-tied

over the sentence and we were all saying it repeatedly with emphasis on the word 'spade'.

During this whole conversation, I noticed Gus, who was resting in my mother's lap—he was tired from chasing the mechanical pool cleaner around—had become intrigued with my mother's repetitious words,

"I used the spade to plant the Scarlet Plumes."

His black-tipped ears dangled as he tilted his head back and forth listening to my mother say,

"I used the spade to plant the Scarlet Plumes."

After she realized that Gus was looking up at her, she said it once more to his curious face while smiling,

"I used the spade to plant the Scarlet Plumes."

We all laughed at his human-like behavior of tilting his head. We all adored his teddy bear qualities, his brown and black fur with his big, round black eyes, which were now wider than ever. Looking at my mother, he immediately perked his ears up, hopped off her lap, disappeared behind the porch, and proceeded to the side yard, where he usually sniffed around for lizards or bugs.

Conversation went on and my mother finished telling us how her day went. My iced tea was now a condensation-drenched glass of ice, so I got up to get some more before dinner. A moment or two went by, just enough for my dad to start inside for another round of beverages, and I went to the garage where we kept an outside refrigerator stocked with beer, soda, and water.

When I stepped inside the garage and flicked on the light, I saw that Gus was already inside. We had a doggie door installed on the garage door, but he never used it unless one of us was about to open it—one of his annoying behaviors. He was already inside the garage so I thought this was odd. He was snooping around the side of the garage when, all of a sudden, I saw him pull something out from behind the dusty croquet set that sat underneath the gardening tools that hung up on the wall.

He brought it over toward me.

He held it in front of me just long enough that I could see what it was, and then he fixed his grasp on it with his mouth and quickly escaped with it through the doggie door.

It was the spade my mother had broken that day! I was astonished. I ran back to the porch, and there was Gus, sitting in front of my mother's feet with the broken spade in his mouth. There hadn't even been five minutes for him to understand what we were talking about before his retrieval. None of us could believe what had happened.

He had only a vague sense of the notion to play fetch. He didn't much care for the game, and so to retrieve an item whose name he had no reason to know was more than incredible. To this day we all joke that Gus understands English. Every now and then he does some amazing things with his own vocal abilities in order to communicate with us, but this was something more!

6 BARKLEY THE BLACK LAB

"Barkley, your LEASH!"

Barkley was part Black Lab, part Australian Shepherd and part Something Small. I found him on my company's intranet one day, from a co-worker who had puppies to give away. I had the idea that I'd "give" him to my husband as a Father's Day present.

But dogs have their own ideas about who "their person" will be. And it's not up to the person!

From the first day, Barkley attached himself to me and me alone. He was 45 pounds of Stubborn Labrador. He was mostly black, but he had a white patch on his chest. The effect was a bit like he was wearing a tuxedo. His bearing reflected that formality and elegance. He was not a clown at all, and he'd turn his nose up at antics. He struck me as a sort of "British" dog, and definitely upscale.

In retrospect, I should have seen what was coming. The first night we took him home and I presented him to my husband as his Father's Day gift, he ignored Hubby and sat at MY feet, put his chin on MY knee, looked up at me adoringly and let us watch television. That settled THAT, as far as who "his human" was going to be!

He was extremely protective of me. Nothing was going to get past him to me—NOTHING. Once I was sitting in a recliner, reading and relaxing. Barkley must have heard something outside. Perhaps it was the mail carrier. My dog started barking ferociously, and then he jumped into my lap, stood at attention (ouch, those nails!) and growled at the invisible person who had not entered the house, but who DARED to walk around outside.

Another time my husband and I were having one of those 'marital discussions' that at times feature voices at slightly elevated volume levels. At one point, my husband must have gestured by waving his hand around. Barkley was not yet initiated into Human Gesture Language, and he interpreted the wave as an act of impending aggression against Best Beloved—me.

He let out a loud and extended warning growl, then ran around me to get behind my husband.

Suffice it to say that heavy denim jeans were not favored by cowboys and the working man for nothing. Nobody was going to raise his hand to me while Barkley was around! When he heard me say "Barkley, no!" he stopped short of ripping the fabric or breaking any skin.

He took a chunk out of the backside of my husband's jeans, by way of firing a warning shot. I said, "Good job, Barks!" He nodded in a most professional and policeman-like way, and walked away slowly.

He stopped once on his way to the kitchen, and gave my husband a look that said, "You watch yourself. I've got my EYES on you!"

That was the day I began nicknaming Barkley "The Best Little Doggie in the Whole Wide World!"

Barkley's protective instincts could sometimes go awry, however.

There was a short set of cement steps leading from the kitchen door to the back garden. One day I had Barkley on his leash and was heading out that kitchen door to take him on his morning walk. I had on one of the capes that I favor in cooler weather. They drape ever so elegantly over the shoulders. The price of this 'elegance' is that they require continual adjustment because they shift around a lot as you wear them. I must have flipped the edge of the cape at precisely the same moment Mr. Barkley decided to take a more emphatic step than usual.

Down the first step I go—and the next thing I know, I'm laid out SPLAT! I'm on the ground below with an intense yowling pain in my left wrist.

Barkley is simply beside himself with worry. To some extent he seems to blame himself because he is as close to hysterical as a canine can get. In his fretfulness, he begins to circle me and start barking in a manner that suggests he is yelling "MAN DOWN, MAN DOWN, NEED HELP STAT!"

The only problem with that is as he circles me in his panic to get me help, he winds his own leash around my neck! In addition to a broken wrist and bruised ribs, now I'm in danger of strangulation by a very upset doggie! Despite all the pain, I could see the humor in the situation, so I began to laugh: felled by a cape, a dog, and a leash. Now I'm gonna DIE! What a way to go!

I was going to be choked to death by an animal who loved me so much he'd gladly throw his little body in front of whatever was coming at me!

As soon as Barkley heard me laughing, he stopped and looked at me. "What?! WHAT!?"

"Barkley, your LEASH!"

Barkley stopped, looked at the leash that was neatly wrapped around my neck. He lay down and put his head between his paws in a sheepish sort of way.

I unwrapped my neck and called 911 because there was no way I was going to be able to drive myself to the hospital.

When I came home and sat down to rest, Barkley never left my side. He'd lie on the floor next to the couch where I'd be resting. Once in a while he'd look at me mournfully: he'd look in my eyes, then look at my broken wrist, then he'd put his head between his paws again and look sad. I would say to him, "Barkley, that's why they call them 'accidents.' Don't worry about it, Buddy." When I'd say that, he'd look up at me, nod, and then go to sleep.

Barkley was like having a small, furry, tuxedoed pal. He was the Pancho Villa to my Don Quixote. He was Gilligan to my Skipper. One of my best memories of my father was watching him with Barkley.

On the fact of it, that might not seem at all unusual, but what you need to know is that my father had a lifelong fear of dogs. He 'hated' them he said. In reality he was scared of them because a large dog jumped on him was he was a small boy. His family were not the type to keep pets, but certainly not dogs.

When Dad saw how Barkley would start barking and growling every time someone unknown got anywhere near me, he'd say, "Nobody's going to bother you as long as HE'S around."

Eventually Barkley impressed my father so much with how gentle he was with me and the family, and how ferocious he could get if he sensed any danger, especially to me. After a few months, I caught my father not only petting Barkley but sneaking him slices of Italian pepperoni, Bark's favorite treat. I'd say "Dad, that stuff is expensive, and Mom wanted it for the pizza!" Dad would look around to see if Mom was near, then shrug his shoulders, grin, and slyly give Barks another slice of pepperoni.

But there were moments.

Something Mr. Barkley did convinced me never to sleep more than two species to a bed.

When Barks was a young dog, an older puppy really, he did something that he never did again. My husband had left a paperback he'd been reading on the coffee table.

Evidently even good dogs get tempted. Barkley picked up the book and chewed it. He chewed it in such a way that most of the novel was still there, but the LAST CHAPTER was gone...

Unfortunately that novel was of the cliffhanger sort. And Barkley chewed off the cliff!

My bedroom at that time was on a lower level of

the house. I had three cats, one dog, and one human (me) in my bedroom. The four-legged family members saw that the two-legged (me) was tired, and they knew the drill.

My husband had been out of the house till later in the evening.

Meanwhile, the three cats, the dog, and I had all climbed into bed.

I remember thinking, before I drifted off to sleep, that I would never have believed that THREE species, two of which were non-human, could co-exist and sleep so peacefully in the same smallish bed.

Until.

I (or we, really) heard the door open. Heard my husband come in.

Then we heard a man YELLING like somebody was sawing off his leg.

"BARRRRRRRKLEYYYYY!!!" He'd seen the chewed paperback. He was not pleased.

The dog flew off the bed first.

As Barkley made for the door (possibly to go 'correct' the male human who'd disturbed the peace), the cats began to fly.

The fat calico went first. She made it out of the bed with no mishaps.

But the white cat had been sleeping on my chest. As she took flight along with the other two domestic beasts, one of her front claws just caught the edge of my ear. She made a neat slice which immediately began to bleed profusely.

As I made my way up the stairs to find out WHAT had caused The Great Pet Bed Exodus, I held a tissue to my ear, which quickly became blood soaked. Barkley saw it, smelled it, and immediately began trying to "herd" me by pushing my legs toward the sofa. Once there, I sat down and my husband (who'd started it with all that yelling) administered first aid. Barks sat, as usual, by my feet, watching us all carefully. As soon as I stopped bleeding, I started petting his head and saying, "I'm OK, Buddy." He got up and went to lie on his dog pillow. He did keep his eyes open though, just to make sure.

His motto was "Never trust a cat or a husband. Because you just never know."

[Cherise's note: Did this one make you laugh as much as it made me laugh? Heh! This is the first of a few stories where the dog is responsible for getting the human into the trouble that the dog later saves the human from. It's sweet that in all cases, the human doesn't seem to notice this. The human is so fond of the dog that he or she blanks out the part about it being the dog who caused the danger. All the focus goes to the dog getting them help for the danger.]

7 SNOWBALL THE PEKINGESE

"Snowball! Go bark at Jan!"

It all started innocently enough. A small white ball of fluff with two round eyes as black as coal stared up at me from the basket.

"He looks like a snowball!" I laughed, and my grandmother agreed.

"You can name him whatever you like, but I think Snowball is a fine name," she said.

And so it was. My grandmother had gotten me the little dog as a surprise for my 12th birthday. I am fairly certain now that she did this without asking my parents for permission, and maybe this was why it was decided that Snowball would reside at my grandmother's apartment with her instead of at my house. But no matter. I spent as much time at her home as I did at my own. Maybe more. And so I was able to see Snowball every day and play with him while Grandma made the roll-away bed up for me to spend the night or fixed supper for me, slipping

Snowball a hot dog or two in the process.

Snowball was the cutest little thing I had ever seen. He ran around the apartment, his toenails clip-clipping on the hardwood floor as he raced from room to room looking for someone to play with ... or maybe more hot dogs! His tail, covered in long fur, curled up over his back most of the time, and his ears were small, soft, and floppy. When he stopped to rest after running or playing, his mouth opened wide into what looked like a big smile as he panted.

But looks can be deceiving.

It turned out that Snowball had a temper. A bad temper. Dare to reach down and take a toy he was playing with, and you might lose a finger. Happen to walk past him when he was in a bad mood, and you might get your ankles chewed. His bark was worse than his bite, however, and he never did any real damage to anyone, but oh, that bark. The little ball of fluff that seemed to smile would suddenly let loose with a ferocious, snarling, growling noise as he shook his head from side to side and chased after you.

But he loved my grandmother and she loved him. I loved him too, but as I grew older I spent less and less time at my grandmother's house, and he became more of her dog than mine. He really had been from the beginning, I suppose. She was the one who walked him and fed him and took care of him. Still, when I moved away to college in warm Arizona and rented a townhouse, I took Snowball with me.

My two-story building had three units in it. Mine was in the middle, and I quickly became friends with an older lady who lived on one side of me. Jan didn't much care for dogs, and quite frankly Snowball didn't care much for Jan. We had adjoining patios and would frequently leave our back doors open and visit each other out back. I left mine open whenever I went out during the day so that Snowball could use my patio to do his business, and Jan kept an eye on my place for me.

But whenever Snowball saw Jan heading our way, he would bark up a storm and growl at her until she ran into her townhouse. I was constantly telling him to be quiet, stop barking, and to be nice, but he just would not listen.

One morning, in a hurry on my way to a job interview, I started down the stairs inside my townhouse and on the second one my foot slipped out from under me and down I went. I tumbled face-forward all the way down the staircase, my legs folded beneath and behind me, stopped only at the bottom by my head crashing into the wall. I lay stunned, certain that I'd broken something, and Snowball hurried to my side. I tried to get up, but it was obvious that my ankle was not going to support me, so I lay back down and envisioned myself having to roll across the house to knock on the wall and hope Jan would come to see what was wrong. It would have been almost comical if my ankle hadn't been hurting so much. Then, a funny idea came to mind.

"Snowball! Go bark at Jan!"

I felt like Timmy asking Lassie to help him out of a mine shaft.

[Cherise's note: Do you remember Lassie? This is the first of a few stories that bring her up. If you aren't old enough to remember, Lassie was a Collie who had her own TV show. Every week she would rescue Timmy from something. She always understood what he said to her. ☺]

Snowball's ears perked up and he whimpered. He had never heard those words before. All he had heard was "Don't bark at Jan." But the next thing I knew he ran to her open door and barked! A few seconds later I heard Jan telling him to pipe down, so I called out to her and she came to the door to see what was wrong. To my surprise, as soon as she came in my door and headed my way, Snowball stopped barking and followed her quietly to me. But as she knelt down and reached out to me, he began to growl softly, just as he did if you reached out to take his toy.

"Snowball … be nice," I said desperately. I didn't want him to attack my rescuer! Again to my surprise, he stopped growling and then settled down on the carpet with his chin resting on his front paws. He stayed that way until Jan got me onto the couch.

He wasn't a changed dog after that. He soon took up barking at Jan again whenever she came over. But for that one day … that one moment when I needed for him to understand me … he did. My little ball of fluff with the big black eyes had understood me.

8 MANDY THE CHIA-POM

Come on, Mandy, do a trick.

My wife and I bought my daughter a puppy several years ago, when my daughter was a young teenager. The fairgrounds in our city have a monthly event where local craftsmen and vendors sell their products and they always have puppies for sale. We took our daughter and she picked out a chia-pom, which is a Chihuahua and Pomeranian mix. She was definitely a cute puppy and she let us cradle her like a baby.

We also bought my son a puppy a few months later, so now we had two puppies in the home. Well, it didn't take long to see who was the dominant dog and who was the smart one. Mandy, our chia-pom, was both. In fact, she is the smartest dog I have ever owned in my life. From the time she set foot in our house, she had the ability to learn things almost immediately.

My daughter said she was going to teach the puppies a few tricks. We had never had a pet that could do tricks, and we had doubts that the puppies could learn anything. Just a few days later, she held up a piece of cheese and told the puppies to beg for it. Immediately Mandy hopped up on her back legs and stayed until she got the treat. The other puppy, Paws, just stood there looking hungry. Shocked at how fast the dog learned, my daughter told us she only showed her one time and she understood. Paws later "got it" but in the meantime, Mandy was learning to do crazy stuff. All you have to do is show the food, motion with your hand what you want her to do and tell her to do it.

Now, Mandy was a bit on the pudgy side, so it was evident that her inspiration was indeed food. She so wanted the cheese treats, that she would zone out everything else to get it. I believe that was the source of her intelligence, the fact that she paid attention to our facial features, our voice inflections, and the fact that she recognized the words we used. She assimilated all of these things quickly.

A typical experience with Mandy would be something like this. "Mandy, cheese?" Mandy would jump on her hind legs and stay there for an eternity. We give her the cheese. "Mandy, roll over." Mandy rolls over and jumps up quickly. I use my finger to indicate rolling over, and say "Mandy" and she rolls over the direction my finger does. I roll my finger the other direction and she rolls over that direction. "Mandy, twirl." I use my finger to indicate an upward spinning motion and she gets on her back legs and starts turning in circles.

One day, we got silly and said, "Mandy, come on, you want some cheese? Come on, Mandy, do a trick."

Mandy proceeded to give us every trick in the book one after another. She started rolling one way, jumped up and went the other, hopped on her back legs and started twirling, and went into some moves that I can't even describe. She actually made them up on the spot. There was never a doubt she understood what we wanted from her. She made us laugh so often, but she did even more.

My daughter went off to college and somehow ended up with another puppy, a lab mix. Long story short, she couldn't keep the puppy where she was, so we inherited her. Her name was Lexie. Lexie grew quickly and acted just like a lab. She loved to fetch, so I would throw her baseballs, rubber footballs, old blankets, chew toys, everything. She would chase it, grab it and lie down with it about 5 feet from me and never give it to me.

Now, keep in mind, Mandy would watch this (we were outside of course) and just sit by my side wanting me to pet her. I asked Lexie,

"Why can't you ever bring the ball back to me?"

So, in a joking manner, I grabbed a nearby stick and threw it about 10 feet the other direction from Lexie, and asked Mandy,

"Mandy, why don't you fetch that stick and bring it to me and we'll show Lexie?"

Now Mandy had NEVER fetched a stick in her

life, because I'd never asked her to. As soon as I said those words, she started walking at a normal pace over to the stick, picked it up, and walked straight back to me and laid it down at my feet. I couldn't believe it. She must have understood what I was asking, there could be no other reason for it. She may have learned from Lexie, but she knew I wanted the stick to be brought to me.

To this day, Mandy and I negotiate over treats.

There is a special area where we let the dogs go to so they don't tromp up the stairs, and we give them a treat to go there. I can close my hand with the treat inside and tell them to go to the area and Paws goes immediately, but Mandy knows, somehow, if the treat is something she likes or doesn't like. Depending on which, she either runs to the area or runs up under the dining room table and 'negotiates'. If I reach in the refrigerator, she starts coming slowly. If I make the cheese wrapper crinkle, she speeds up. If I grab something else, she retreats. She's just so smart.

My favorite saying, regarding her, is "Mandy is the second smartest one in this house." That always gets the family to arguing who is number one.

9 TREBLE THE YORKIE

"Have you seen Mom?" Lily asked.

My mother decided over breakfast to take our Yorkie to the groomers. Treble lay under the table, patient in her quest for scraps. Her tail shifted every so often on the hardwood floor and her lips pulled back to give the impression of a smile.

Treble's smile changed fast when she heard The Word. "I'm taking Treble to be groomed," Mom said, and took a sip of orange juice.

Treble let out a low whine. She stood up and took off down the hallway. My sister and I laughed.

"She's not going now," I said.

Mom sighed, exasperated. "She'll go."

"You shouldn't have said it out loud," Maggie said. "You know she knows that word."

Treble has lived with us since she was a puppy. Since then, we've taught her all kinds of words. Some, like grooming, she picked up on her own.

Mom nodded. "Well, we'll just have to cheer her

up again before we go."

After breakfast, Lily and I sought out Treble. Lily checked the basement. I went upstairs to the bedrooms. I found Treble curled up with some slippers under my parents' bed.

"Hey girl," I said, in a soft cooing voice.

Treble looked at me but did not budge.

It took me a moment but I thought of a new plan, a game that Treble loves. My voice took on an excited yet worried tone when I spoke to her next.

"I can't find Lily," I said. "Where is she?"

Treble's ears perked up. She squirmed out from under the bed and barked once. It was as if she was saying she was on the job. Treble raced through the door and down the stairs. I followed her to the main floor and then to the basement door. She scratched at the wood with one eager paw, turning her head to give me a look of impatience.

I opened the door for her and she shot down the stairs. I heard the bark of excitement that meant she had found Lily. Lily laughed and greeted the Yorkie. "We're playing 'Where is?'" I called to her.

Lily appeared at the bottom of the stairs.

"Oh no," she said, and looked around.

Treble, coming up next to her, swiveled her head to follow where Lily was looking.

"I can't find Squirrel. Where is she?"

Treble took off, ready for the next hunt. Lily

bounded up the stairs and we followed our little dog on her new quest, eager to see if she found the right toy. Treble's basket of toys sat in the corner of the living room, all of them sprawled together like a diverse litter of puppies. Lily and I caught up to Treble as she was nosing through her collection, searching for the missing squirrel. She tugged a stuffed raccoon out of the mess, and tossed it aside. She flung a rope knot toy over the side of the woven wooden basket. Then she found her. The missing squirrel.

I knelt beside the basket and Treble placed the squirrel in my lap. She looked up at Lily with wide, proud eyes. Her tongue panted and her lips were back to making that smiling impression.

"Thanks, Treble," Lily said, and reached down to pet Treble's head.

My eyes scanned the basket. "Hey Lily."

"Yeah?"

"Birdie is missing."

Treble did not even wait for us to ask where Birdie was, she simply took off. She went back upstairs, to Lily's room. She'd gone to bed there last night, the Birdie cuddled tight to her chest. We waited for her to grab the pale yellow bird from Lily's bed and return to the living room. When she appeared at the top of the stairs we began our praise. Her tail wagged fiercely back and forth. She dropped the bird at Lily's feet.

"Good girl," I repeated, scratching Treble's neck just behind her ears. She yipped with pleasure and beat her tail even more furiously.

"Have you seen Mom?" Lily asked.

"Why no, I haven't," I said.

Treble sat down and lifted her ears. After a few moments of intense listening, she jogged to the garage door and pressed a paw against it. She barked, and we obeyed. We opened the door for her, and the three of us spilled into the garage.

Mom was getting the van ready to go. She laid a blanket across the middle seat and put the box of treats up front. When we entered the garage she turned to us and smiled.

"Ah, so you did manage to cheer her up," she said.

"Yeah," Lily and I chorused.

Mom knelt down to pet Treble's curly fur. "You're such a good girl," Mom said, and kissed her head.

"It's time to go, Treble. Get your ball and meet me in the car."

Treble ran out the open garage door to the front lawn. Her tennis ball was nestled in the grass. She grasped it between her teeth and did a few sprints around the yard, pausing once to go to the bathroom.

She did not forget Mom's command. Ball still in her mouth, she trotted back to the garage and hopped into the van. Lily and I piled in after her and pulled the door shut.

When your dog speaks English, it is hard to keep secrets from her. The good thing, though, is that when she is upset, communication makes it easier to cheer her up.

10 RANCHITO BANDITO THE BORDER COLLIE

All the rabbits are out! I need your help!

When I was growing up, my family had a beautiful long haired, black-and-white Border Collie. Her name was Ranchito Bandito or Ranch Bandit, but we just called her Bandit. I grew up on a farm in the middle of nowhere and she was my constant companion. At times she was my best friend, and I know that she could understand what I was saying.

The first time I started wondering if Bandit could understand me was when I was out on a trail ride with a friend. We were riding our horses along a creek with the plan of having a picnic up the trail a few miles by the reservoir. Bandit and I had gone ahead a little ways when my horse started spooking. He wouldn't move any farther up the trail. Just up the way a bit was a humongous rattle snake. I yelled back to my friend, "Rattler!" and that is when Bandit perked up.

She started pacing the trail in front of me, head held low and growling all the while in the direction of the snake.

When my friend finally caught up, we sat there for a while discussing our options. We had been looking forward to this ride for weeks. Neither one of us wanted to turn back, but with the way the terrain was in that area, we could not go around. The snake was blocking our only path to our destination. My friend suggested that we should just wait and it would eventually move on.

"Maybe the dog will scare it off," I said.

Bandit just looked at me and then went into a frenzy. She ran up the trail barking, lunging at the snake and dodging away from it, snarling and snapping. She kept up this tirade for about ten minutes until the snake finally gave in and slithered away.

Living on the farm meant animals, and lots of them. My sister and I had very expensive champion show rabbits that we would also breed. One hot summer day, I was relaxing under the apple tree with Bandit lying nearby when I saw one of the rabbits across the lawn. He was very tame and munching happily on a patch of clover, so I was easily able to catch him. I walked into the rabbit shed to put him away and realized all of the rabbits were gone! We still have no idea how, but all of their cages were open!

I ran into the house with Bandit on my heels and called downstairs to my sister,

"All the rabbits are out! I need your help!"

The dog turned around and shot back out the front door. When I ran back outside she had her head low to the ground, sniffing. She suddenly darted into the brush and came out the other side chasing one of the rabbits! She herded it toward me and cornered it by the front porch. My sister scooped it up and took back to the shed. Bandit sat there waiting at my feet. I patted her on the head and said,

"Good job! Go find another one!"

and off she went. In two hours of running and sniffing (her poor nose had to be exhausted!), she managed to find and round up every single one of the twenty missing rabbits.

[Cherise's note: I just love that a dog is out there herding rabbits! Don't you wish you could have seen that? I wonder if she was thinking, 'Yum, these smell so good! I sure wish I were hunting them instead of eating them. Maybe I can eat just one? No, better not. The humans seem mighty attached to them, almost like young. Ooh! There's another one!']

Another morning I was out doing my daily chores, walking along a path that I had walked a thousand times before. I suddenly felt a sharp stab in the arch of my foot. I quickly sat down and took my boot off. I had a huge gash in my foot with a piece of metal embedded deep in my arch. A metal fence post had apparently broken off many years ago below the surface of the ground and I had put just enough pressure in the right spot that it pressed up through the ground, through my boot, and into my foot. I tried to stand and limp toward the house but my foot couldn't support any weight. I tried calling for help, but no one could hear me. My mom and sister had gone to town, and my dad was out in the lower fields doing irrigation.

Bandit was whining and shoving her head under my arm. She was so worried. I suppose I should have known by now that she was smarter than the average dog, but I jokingly told her,

"Go get Dad!"

I fully expected to have to crawl back to the house by myself. She cocked her head to the side as if to check to make sure she understood me correctly, and then off she ran. I could hear her in the distance a few minutes later, barking up a storm. Pretty soon, here comes my dad being led by Bandit! He helped get pressure on my foot to stop the bleeding and got me back to the house.

Later, he told me how Bandit ran out in front of his truck and started barking. He tried to quiet her and shoo her out of the way but she would not budge. When my dad finally stepped out of the truck, he said that the dog ran up, grabbed his hand in her mouth, and started tugging him back toward the sheep pen, toward me. He gave in and followed her and I'm so very glad he did. That was the last time I ever doubted that Bandit knew exactly what I was saying. She was the smartest dog I have ever met!

11 BUDDY THE BLACK LAB

*It's a school of fish, Buddy, just like the
one I caught.*

One cold evening in late December, I arrived home
to find an extremely large black Labrador Retriever
lying on my front porch. At first I was hesitant to get
out of my car, fearing he might be an aggressive dog.
After sitting in my car and contemplating my options,
I decided I had no choice but to get out and make my
way to my front door. As the car door opened, the
dog slowly raised his head in my direction. This made
me a bit nervous, so I slowly approached with my
hand out, just to let him know I meant no harm. The
dog's tail wagged vigorously and he made his way
over to me with his head hung low. I patted his head
as I spoke to him.

"Are you lost, Buddy?" I said.

He simply laid his big head in my hand, and my heart melted.

I decided he must be someone's dog. Immediately, I planned my course of action. Tomorrow, I would run an ad in the paper and see if anyone claimed this gentle giant. For the time being, he needed a name, so I called him Buddy.

The following day, I placed the ad and waited. After seven days, there was no response and I decided that Buddy would be my dog. Each day when I got home from work, Buddy would jump up and meet me at my car with what seemed to be a smile on his face. He really was a sweet creature and loved the time we spent together. After several months passed, I was due for a vacation and I decided Buddy and I should take a trip down to the lake.

The next day I packed the car with all of our supplies and off we went on our first adventure together. Buddy seemed to be more excited about this trip than I had imagined. He hung his head out the window as the wind whipped his hair and floppy ears. As we arrived at the lake, his ears shot straight up and he sat at attention. Buddy shot out of the car and ran like a maniac around the lake. He chased birds, ran in the water, and barked at fish—all within the first two minutes of our arrival. As I finished unpacking, he made his way back over to me and lay down. He seemed to have worn himself out and was ready for a nap.

By the time I had finished unpacking all of our things, it was nearing evening, and the sun was setting low over the lake. Buddy watched with intent as it sank lower in the horizon, and only when it was out of site did he lay his head back upon his feet. I could tell he loved it here and was right at home in these surroundings. After some time spent around the campfire, eating and relaxing, I unzipped the tent and called to Buddy. He got up and made his way over to the tent, but refused to go inside. He was resigned to lie at the opening of the tent and see all of his surroundings. Finally, I agreed and settled in for the night.

The next morning, as soon as I made my way out of the tent, Buddy took off again, making his crazed rounds around the lake, chasing the birds and barking at the water. I had to laugh as I grabbed the fishing poles and tackle and set up in front of our campsite. I placed the rods in the rod holders and sat down in my chair and waited. Buddy continued his morning rounds until he again wore himself out. He made his way over to our makeshift fishing area and flopped down with a thud. Not long after, I got my first bite.

Buddy jumped as I ran over to grab my pole. I reeled with intention until I had the fish on the landing. Buddy was more than excited and tried to run off with my fish. I commanded him,

"Drop it,"

and like the obedient dog he was, he did so, right at my feet.

Buddy was the kind of dog that made your heart smile. He aimed to please in everything he did, and so often I felt like he understood every word I spoke to him. I placed my first fish in the cooler and Buddy sniffed and examined our trophy. I explained to him that was our fish and our supper for this evening. He seemed content with the explanation and slowly made his way back to his sleeping spot by the poles. After some time, I noticed a dark spot in the lake that seemed to be moving towards us. The water whirled and moved and ever so slowly made its way about thirty feet from the shore. Immediately, Buddy's ears shot up and he looked at me with a question behind his eyes.

"It's a school of fish, Buddy, just like the one I caught," I said.

Before I knew what had happened, Buddy went like a streak of lightning to the water. He didn't stop at the water's edge but continued straight towards the school of fish. Just when I was beginning to think he had lost his mind, he dove under the water and to my amazement came up, having caught in his mouth the biggest trout I'd ever seen!

He understood my words so he caught his own supper.

The rest of the day Buddy and I caught fish. At evening I cleaned them all and we sat down to the largest feast I ever had. Buddy enjoyed his share too. After 3 days, we made our way home and even had fish to freeze for another meal. I'm not sure who enjoyed that vacation more, me or Buddy, but I do know I had found the best fishing partner to ever walk on four legs.

12 TASHA THE GERMAN SHEPHERD

When you get lonely and want to see him,
come to this spot.

The day was August 28, 2011. It was a sad day for my family members and for me as well. My father had passed away at the age of 41 unexpectedly due to a clot in his Aorta. It was hard to understand and deal with.

I was at the hospital and had left my German Shepherd Tasha alone all day. She was probably getting worried and wondering why my father and I hadn't come home yet. She would always wait for us, and the second she'd see our vehicle, she would start carrying on; barking, jumping, and wagging that bushy tail of hers. I could only imagine what she would think when she only saw me coming inside alone and not with my father. He'd never spent a night without Tasha, since the day he got her. She'd always been by his side.

They always say that a man's best friend is his dog, and in this case it was the truth. I remember growing up, wherever my father was Tasha was right there next to him. Tasha thought she was a lap dog, so every time my father would relax on the couch, she would be right on his lap. German Shepherds are not small dogs, and her thinking she was a smaller dog amused me.

When I came home from the hospital, I was emotional and I was alone. I was always by myself if my father wasn't home. The only company I received daily was from Tasha. When I came home that night to Tasha she could tell that something was wrong, and something was missing in the house. She went exploring around the house, looking for something.

Then it came to me. She was looking for my father and wondering why he hadn't come home with me. An hour passed by and Tasha was staring at the door, whimpering. It was heart breaking watching her watch the front door, listening for the garage door, and looking out the windows. Every little sound that she heard, she would get excited and start wagging her tail and barking, then once a few minutes passed by she would hang her head low and go back to her waiting spot. It was devastating to watch, and made my heart break even more.

I went to bed to try and ease my pain and forget about what had happened for a little while. I noticed that Tasha did not follow me up; instead she went and slept on my father's bed. She did not understand what was going on. This was when I knew I had to take the time in the morning to have a talk with her to try and help her understand.

When that morning came I woke up to a call from

the hospital stating my father's ashes were ready for pick up. I got up and I made myself a breakfast, French toast to be exact. I made Tasha some too so we could enjoy breakfast together, like she and my father always had, but she barely ate. I could tell she was down and needed some cheering up, so I took her with me.

I went into the hospital and got my father's ashes, put them in the back seat of the car, and then I took Tasha to the park. I wanted Tasha to have a good day, before I had to break the news to her about my father's passing. I grabbed us an ice cream cone each. She had vanilla and I had chocolate. I walked her over to a bench and we sat down. I told her how good of a dog she was, and that she will always be loved, no matter what. Then we got into the car and headed home.

Once we got home I created a memorial for my father. It had his picture, ashes, handprints, and quilt. I brought Tasha to this memorial and simply stated to her, "He is gone, and he will not be returning. No matter how bad we want him to walk through that door, it will not happen. He is in a better place, and his remains are in this Urn."

"When you get lonely and want to see him, come to this spot. He will help you."

I didn't know if she could understand what I was saying until she laid her head in my lap looking up at my father's memorial, whimpering. I knew at that very moment she understood what I was saying to her, and that she would be OK. This was the day that I learned my German Shepherd could understand English.

Once Tasha learned that my father was no longer coming back, her appetite came back. She started eating more and the whimpering came to an end. Every now and then I will catch her lying under my father's memorial fast asleep. It amazes me what a dog can comprehend when it comes to the English language. People always say they talk to their dogs about complications because they can't understand, but I think dogs understand a lot more than we think.

[Cherise's note: I lost my own father last year. I had a sister to mourn with, so I feel blessed. I feel so sad for this person who only had a dog, but what a perfect dog to mourn with. I love how Tasha and the human mourn together. This is how I wish the saying 'Misery loves company' always played out: two with a common loss commiserating and helping each other mourn. This story is beautiful to me. I hope you got something out of it, too.]

13 MITZY THE GERMAN SHEPHERD

*Watch out for snakes, Mitz. Call me if
these kids don't behave!*

Mitzy is our three year old German Shepherd. She is playful and loves our children; she is their greatest protector (next to Mom and Dad of course). She responded early to normal commands, but we never had her formally trained. I sometimes take for granted her protection, loyalty, and love—she gives it so freely.

The summer weather in the mountains of Eastern Kentucky can be a bit erratic. Some days the kids and I enjoy a swim in the pool when the July heat and humidity melts even the coldest Popsicle in record time. Other days we spend inside watching a movie or playing dress-up while the rain pours down, leaving our yard a swamp. Some days I expect to see an alligator just hanging out by the mailbox. So with humid mornings and sporadic downpours in the afternoons, we have not had the greatest weather for enjoying the outdoors. When we do get a pleasant day outside, we take full advantage: me, the kids, and Mitzy.

Our back yard is on a steep slope lined with trees and brush. This is Mitzy's favorite spot. It provides her with some shade, a place to run, and a never ending game of pushing a ball up the hill with her nose then chasing it when it rolls back down. The hill is too steep for the kids to play on. My oldest, Hunter, is six and my daughter, Harper, just turned four. At the top of the hill is our deck with a pool and barbeque area. Hunter and Harper love playing in the pool and then sitting on the concrete to play in the sand box. Occasionally Mitzy makes the trek up the hill with her ball to roll around in the sand with them and then jump in the pool, leaving me with a nice sandy mess to clean up after.

One afternoon Mitzy was basking in the shade while the kids were busy building sandcastles. I had swept and cleaned around the deck and was going inside to quickly wash our dishes from lunch. Before going inside I told them, like I had at least a million times, to watch out for snakes. Even though the only snake we had seen around the house was a baby snake not much bigger than a worm (several months earlier), I always tell them to keep an eye out. I have a slight phobia of snakes to say the least.

I called down to Mitzy, "Watch out for snakes, Mitz. Call me if these kids don't behave!"

Harper laughed. "Mommy, Mitzy doesn't even have a phone. She can't call you!"

"She's asleep anyway. She didn't hear you." Hunter chimed in.

The kitchen window directly faces where the kids were sitting. I opened the window so I could talk back and forth with them. I listened to them debating which cartoon they would watch when it was time to come inside. When I was drying the last glass, I heard Mitzy.

I looked out the window and she was at the bottom of the hill looking up towards the kids. This was not her usual bark. These were loud spaced out sounds with long pauses between her "words" for lack of a better term. She sounded like she was speaking in Morse code. I didn't see anything or anyone around so I stuck the glasses in the cupboard and headed outside. When I stepped out onto the lower deck, Mitzy had already climbed the hill and was heading for the pool. I thought she must have gotten too hot and needed to take a dip.

She jumped in and jumped out. Then she went over to the sand where Hunter and Harper were and shook her fur out to dry. They think it's funny that Mitzy acts as their personal sprinkler on hot days. After shaking herself dry, Mitzy ran back to the pool and jumped in again. This time she stayed in and barked her usual playful bark as she paddled along. The kids decided to swim too so they both hopped in to splash with her. It was hot and I was caught up on chores for the moment, so I decided that a quick swim sounded like a good idea. The second I cleared the ladder, Mitzy jumped out and rushed over to the hill. I assumed that she was going to get her ball.

I was wrong. Mitzy barreled past her ball and stopped in the shade just in front of the trees. She had piqued our curiosity, so the kids and I peered over the edge of the pool to see what she was doing. She lowered her head to the ground, picked up something in her mouth and turned to come back up the hill. As she climbed closer I realized it was a snake! I was petrified. Should we stay in the pool? Should we try and run into the house?

When Mitzy got closer, I could tell that the snake was dead. A slight relief to me, but even a dead snake is a snake, and I wanted nothing to do with it. When she reached the top of the hill, she carried the snake to the farthest corner of the concrete and dropped it out of her mouth. She then started to bark in the "Morse code" bark again.

My husband was at work and I wasn't going near the snake, so I shuffled the kids out of the pool, ran inside and called a neighbor for snake removal duty. When the neighbor arrived I recounted the story of Mitzy killing the snake and leaving it at the bottom of the hill before she ushered us all to safety in the pool.

Maybe I read too much into her actions, but I truly feel that Mitzy has taken to heart the "watch for snakes" advice that I have reiterated to my kids so many times.

14 SAM THE GOLDEN LAB

Jump in, Sweetie.

I've had the very same dog for almost 7 years now and she is the only dog I've owned that I really believe can understand what I'm saying. It has been this way since I got her, when she was 7 months old.

Sam (short for Samantha) is a golden lab that I picked up from a friend who was looking for a home for the runt of the litter. I fell in love with her the moment she decided to lick my cheek when I picked her up. I took her home with the expectation of having to go through a lot of hard work, which turned out to be completely wrong. Sam is a very smart dog and responds to what is being requested of her as long as it is delivered in the right tone and especially when it comes from me.

I first started wondering if Sam could understand what I was saying in the first week that I had her home with me. I live in a two story town house and we were hanging out downstairs watching TV.

When the movie ended, I looked at Sam and said,

"Let's go upstairs now, Sweetie."

She literally rolled off the couch and climbed up the stairs before I even got off the couch. This was only the first incident that made me think she understood what I was saying.

A few days later I was in the kitchen making a sandwich and Sam was looking up at me like she wanted something but I knew that she had already eaten her food so she couldn't be hungry. I wasn't sure what it was she wanted so I simply asked, "Do you have to go potty?" and without even hesitating, she ran to the front door and stood there waiting. I hadn't begun using the term 'potty' yet. I believe she just understood me.

One of the most amazing situations I remember in the earlier days with Sam was a time when we had come back from PetSmart and I had just opened the car door to let Sam out. I noticed that I had forgotten to pick up one of the newspapers off the lawn, so I thought I'd make a joke and test my theory out once again. I simply said, "Sam, go get the paper," and wouldn't you know it, she actually went over to the paper and tried to pick it up. Unfortunately, it wouldn't work because she couldn't get her mouth around it but she really gave it a good try.

Sam has never had a problem understanding what I was saying and this even applied to basic commands. It usually took one try to get her to listen to a command and it was really impressive. It took one single attempt at telling her to 'come' and she ran over and jumped up onto the chair with me. The same went for the opposite situation when I told her 'down' and she jumped off the chair. I have been around many other dogs and don't know of a single one that understands (or listens for that matter) as well as Sam does.

As she got older, Sam seemed to just get smarter with the things that she understood. It was easy teaching Sam to do what most dog owners consider to be tricks. I consider them simply understanding and listening to a command. She learned to shake, roll over, and beg on the second attempt at worst each time. I have a friend who trains dogs who didn't believe me until she tried a slightly difficult command that Sam picked up almost immediately.

At the park, Sam is the center attraction almost every time. From the day she could run fast enough to fetch, all it took was throwing an item and walking her over to it while saying, "Fetch." Each time after that, she would do the job on her own. She now catches a Frisbee in the air. The first time we went to a lake and I encouraged her to jump in for a swim by saying,

"Jump in, Sweetie,"

she did just that.

She even listens to other people, but only if they speak in the right tone, though. They have to speak as if they expect her to understand, not in a sing-songy teasing way like they feel embarrassed to be speaking to her. I'm pretty sure she understands anyone speaking. She will, however, only listen to those she wants to listen to.

Today Sam is smarter than she has ever been and would sit and talk to me if she could only talk. She really does enjoy listening to people talk to her and the expressions on her face are amazing. I recently adopted another female lab named Krissy that is 2 years old and it's funny how Sam will attempt to coax her into listening to commands I give to the two of them together. Sam will sit for a minute staring at Krissy as if to say, "Why aren't you doing what you were told?" It even looks like Sam is trying to teach Krissy what to do with commands as they are given.

Having a dog as smart as Sam around this long has been a great experience for both of us. She really does understand what I am saying and I really believe this. We'll just have to see if she has any luck teaching Krissy how to understand English as well.

[Cherise's note: Our dogs respond best when we just talk to them as if we expect them to understand, too. My head tells me they read body language that we don't even know we're using, like the horse Clever Hans. Read about him on Wikipedia if you don't know the story. It's fascinating. However, my heart tells me our dogs are just as intelligent as we are, but they just cannot communicate with us. That is the premise of my dog aliens novels.]

15 MAGGIE, MY AUSTRALIAN SHEPHERD

Initially I used words like 'walk', 'turn left', and 'turn right' to get her through the course.

I was a teenager when I got Maggie. My mom knew that I wanted a dog and she had a friend bring over three puppies that were about six weeks old. Two of the puppies were reddish brown with mottled white coloring. They were playful, friendly and very cute. The other puppy was gray and black and white and she had one blue eye. She sat near me and watched me play with her brother and sister.

She didn't demand attention but was content just to be next to me. That was what really got my attention. My mom asked me if I had a favorite. I picked her up and said, "This one" as I held this sweet puppy to my face and gave her a kiss. My mom said, "She's yours! What will you name her?" I was shocked that my mom had just given me such a wonderful surprise. I named her Maggie and she learned her name right away.

Maggie was very quick to learn new things. It seemed like all I had to do was tell her something a couple of times and she knew exactly what I wanted. It was in her heart to please me. When she got big enough, we went to Obedience School. I knew that it was important for her to understand basic commands such as Sit – Stay – Lie Down. Maggie breezed through Obedience School with no problems.

Maggie was an Australian Shepherd, which is a working dog. This breed of dogs is very smart and they like to be challenged. My mom suggested that I start teaching her how to maneuver different obstacles in a dog agility course. These courses are competitive events and they are a lot of fun. We had several horses who worked similar courses, and so I worked with my dad to build different pieces for a dog agility course.

The purpose of the course is to see how well a dog can follow commands and show assertiveness—and to make the crowd clap and cheer. We built a Pole Weave by cutting PVC pipe into five equal lengths of three feet. We drilled holes into a longer section of PVC pipe and then glued the 3' sections into the holes. We put T-Connectors on the ends of the longer pipe so that it would stand up.

I worked with Maggie, teaching her how to bend around each vertical section of pipe.

Initially I used words like 'walk', 'turn left', and 'turn right' to get her through the course.

Eventually, she learned to go through the poles just by watching me raise my hand and point to the object.

It was a good thing she already knew basic commands before we started because she wanted to run the course over and over. My dad and I worked on building other pieces for the course so that she would continue to learn and not get bored.

We built a see-saw that she would walk up from one end, cross over the center and then continue to walk as the other end came down from her weight. I worked with her for a couple of days on this because she had to focus on the task and not jump off the see-saw. I taught her a new word, 'Wait'. I wanted her to balance on the center of the see-saw so that the board was centered horizontally.

As she learned each new obstacle we were already working on building the next one. Maggie loved to jump and catch a Frisbee so we used this natural ability on the obstacle course. We built a stand that held a large Hula-hoop. I would have her sit-stay about 10 feet from the hoop and then tell her 'Jump the Hoop'. She would dash over and jump right through the center of the hoop. She loved it even more when I threw a Frisbee for her to chase through the hoop.

I went to a dog show to see what other obstacles people were using to teach their dogs new skills. We discovered something called the 'King of the Hill Ramp'. This is an A-frame obstacle with horizontal slats on the ramp to help the dog climb. The dog starts by climbing up one side of the ramp, pauses at the top of the A-frame and then continues down the other side. The hard part was to teach Maggie not to jump from the top of the obstacle. The commands, 'Stay and Wait' were very useful in training for this part of the course. She always wanted to jump from the top and then run in circles. It was funny to see her do this because she seemed to be smiling, but I had to be stern and make her stay on task so that she would finish the obstacle correctly.

When Maggie was a few years old, my sister got a new dog. The new dog was not a good influence on Maggie and she tested me, much like a teenager does with their parents.

I would come home from school and the garbage can in the kitchen would be overturned and the contents strung out all over the kitchen and living room.

I would look at Maggie, point to my bedroom and say, "Go to your room." Maggie would tuck her tail between her legs and slink off to my room. I didn't have to yell at her or tell her that she was bad. She knew it. She was a very social dog, so being banished to the bedroom was punishment that she didn't like.

Eventually I took Maggie with me whenever I rode my horses out into the desert. She would get really excited and stand on her back legs and put her paws on the shoulder of my horse. She just loved going out, and she never ran off. She was a very good dog and very obedient.

16 HONCHO THE
CHIHUAHUA/AIREDALE TERRIER

*My roommates have been amazed that
when they said, "Blake's coming home,"
or "I hear Blake outside," his ears perk
up and he starts looking around happily.*

Honcho is a good boy and a wonderful companion.
He is currently 10 years old and I have owned him for
6 years of his life. He is a genuine mutt, but
genetically his mother was a Chihuahua and his father
was an Airedale Terrier.

Honcho has many fine qualities, but his best traits
are that he does not bark a lot, he is good at guarding
the house, and he gets along very well with my 3 cats.
Honcho is younger than 2 of my cats named Mouser
and Maggie, but 4 years older than my littlest calico
named Piper. All my animals live with me in the
United States, but Honcho has another special talent

as an American pet.

My dog Honcho not only understands many English words, but I have done my best to keep his bilingual upbringing. He was previously owned by three different families in my area. The first spoke Spanish, the second spoke English and the third spoke Spanish to Honcho. The family that had him before I did, they were going to have him put to sleep. They couldn't keep him and would have taken him to the dog pound, but I offered to take him instead.

When I adopted him, it was my decision to keep his Spanish name. It seemed that he responded to it, so I didn't want to confuse him any more than he already had been, having so many different owners. Plus I was not sure if Honcho was smart, so speaking 2 languages couldn't hurt. It turned out that Honcho was very smart and a loyal dog companion.

Now I think of him as my best friend.

His name actually is a source of great fun. Honcho knows his own name, but also responds to my playful way of calling him the Head Honcho. That is what I will tell him he is before leaving the house for any extended period of time. Since I am the head of the household, he is the Head Honcho in my absence. When I return home, I tell him he is a good Honcho Poncho. Honcho Poncho is the nickname I started calling him to let him know that I was home to stay a while.

But Honcho's response to English words is much more interesting.

The first and most obvious word he responded to was my name, Blake.

My roommates have been amazed that when they said, "Blake's coming home," or "I hear Blake outside," his ears perk up and he starts looking around happily.

I never tried to teach him my name, but he seemed to pick it up on his own. I guess I am his Blake.

He also knows the names of my cats and responds to their names differently. Mouser is a boy cat and likes Honcho a lot. When Honcho hears the name Mouser, he always jumps in a circle and gets ready to play. When Honcho hears the name Maggie, he knows that he needs to be on his best behavior. This is because Maggie is an old lady cat and does not like to play rough. Finally when Honcho hears the name Piper, he usually moves out of the way. Although Piper likes to play, Honcho usually ends up with her smacking him in the nose or worse. Piper likes it, but Honcho not so much.

He responds to both Spanish and English words for basic commands. Since the word 'no' translates into either language, it was the easiest command to get him to understand. He knew what it meant immediately, so I guess it was something he heard a lot with his former owners.

He initially did not respond to the words 'yes' or 'good', but he did understand 'si' and 'bueno'. It took a little time, but eventually he showed signs that he was responding to and understanding these new words.

I try never to use the word 'bad' with him, so I can't say if it is in his dog vocabulary. Instead of telling him he's bad, I started saying the phrase "Run for your life." I say it loudly and let him know that he is doing something mischievous. If he is caught really doing something wrong, I will add a stomping foot on the floor with it. Either way, "Run for your life" always gets him to race outside. Then Honcho waits until I let him know that he may come back inside. I do this by telling him he is a "Good Honcho."

Other interesting phrases he seems to understand have happened slowly over time. Keep in mind that I did not become Honcho's owner until he was nearly 4 years old, so it is amazing that I was able to train him to understand any new words or commands. In my opinion, he is very smart that way.

[Cherise's note: I don't buy the idea that 'you can't teach an old dog new tricks.' I can't count how many times I heard this growing up, and I used to believe it, but I don't anymore. We'd had our Border Collie / Springer Spaniel Oreo six years before he finally stopped pulling on the leash. Most of the time. He still sometimes gets over excited when he sees a squirrel. That just proves that the change in his behavior is a learned one and not a symptom of his being aged.]

[Cherise's funny side note: I was discussing Oreo's behavior with a vet friend the other day. He asked if Oreo is obsessive, and said he's known Border Collies who tried to herd shoes or dust motes.
I said, "No, Oreo is more of a hunter. He can't resist chasing squirrels and birds, and he barks while he chases them... Hm... Maybe Oreo is trying to herd the birds and squirrels!"
That made the vet laugh, and he said, "Possibly!"]

Honcho knows the difference between the words 'TV' and 'radio'.

When I say anything like "Let's watch TV," he runs to his favorite leather chair in the living room. It is close enough to the television set that he can watch it, but it's far enough away that he can still look around at anything else going on in the immediate vicinity.

In contrast, when I say something like "Turn up the radio," he will run to his favorite floor pillow that sits near my bass woofer. He loves the thumping sound and seems to like reggae music, punk rock and anything with horns playing in it.

There is one word that Honcho does not like, but he definitely understands it when he hears it. That word is 'vet'. I am not sure he knows 'veterinarian', but he does know that 'vet' is the same as 'Doctor Garcia'. Saying either one will cause Honcho to hide in my bedroom closet, or sometimes the backyard shed. I guess it is because he gets his shots regularly, so he thinks about that when he hears either 'Doctor Garcia' or the 'vet'.

I hate doing it, but now instead I say, "Does Honcho want to ride with Blake?" which he knows means going for a ride in the car, one of his all-time favorite things to do. I hate having to trick him, so when we finish visiting the veterinarian, I always take him to the dog park for a reward.

He really is a good dog and I am so lucky to have him. Honcho is my good boy, the Head Honcho and my Honcho Poncho. The dog who knows English and Spanish too.

17 DUKE THE GOLDEN RETRIEVER

Dad is on an airplane. He's not coming
back for a couple of days.

When I was growing up, I had a Golden Retriever named Duke. He had an uncanny knack for knowing things, even when he was a young pup and still learning all the strange ways of us humans. He caught on within a day of newspaper training that newspapers were for peeing on, which was too bad for us because it took us longer than a day to remember that we could not set the day's newspaper on the floor anymore. Fortunately, he caught on to the last part of housebreaking quickly too and maybe even figured out that our praise was far more genuine if he asked to go outside than if he marked the day's sports section.

So he started as a good, smart puppy and grew into a good, smart young dog. Commands were not his strong point but he had an amazing vocabulary for things. He mastered the word for walk, so we had to say 'W'. Then he learned 'W', so we had to just accept that the walk would happen as soon as somebody requested he get a walk, because nobody could resist his pleas. The same thing happened with car rides, treats, and his favorite command, 'Come with'. Wherever anyone was invited, Duke was invited if somebody made the mistake of using that phrase. He made sure of that.

He was also familiar with the command 'Get Bone', which meant he had to go back to wherever he had left his bone outside and bring it back in with him. Golden Retrievers do not have the same digging instincts as a terrier breed, but they feel more comfortable with something in their mouth. Duke always had to bring something outside with him when he went out to play. Usually it was a bone, but sometimes it was a scrap of cardboard he dug out of the recycling, and once in a while it was a ball, but there had to be something he could fit in his mouth when he went outside.

Without the 'Get Bone' command, this habit would have yielded rawhide bones scattered all over the yard and deck. Many times it did anyway because somebody would let him into the house without his bone. Whenever he ran out of bones in the house we would have to bring them back in for him, otherwise the poor dog would scurry around the house, looking for anything to put in his teeth while we stood at the door waiting for him to find his chosen toy.

By the time he was two years old, he had advanced from 'Get Bone', to 'Get Squirrel'. If somebody looked outside and said casually,

"Hey Duke, Squirrel Alert. Go get it,"

Duke would get to his feet and run out the door—
no need for toys on this trip—and find the tree with
the squirrel and bark and bark and bark. He knew
what we meant from the first time I tried it. Maybe he
smelled the squirrel, or maybe all the chicken we were
feeding him had enlarged his brain, but really none of
us quite figured out exactly how he learned the
English word for squirrel.

The most impressive vocabulary feat, however,
was when he taught himself the meaning of the word
'airplane'. An airplane is a tiny speck in the sky. They
make a faint noise but our house was far enough from
the airport that even for a dog it could not have been
very noticeable. There certainly was no scent. But
Duke knew about airplanes. He learned the word, and
he hated them worse than squirrels.

It all started because he was deeply devoted to my
dad. We would joke that Duke was my dad's extra
four legs because Duke would follow him almost
anywhere. My dad often had to take trips for work,
and he would fly out of town, leaving Duke to mope
by the stairs, waiting for him to come back. I pitied
Duke and would sit there, stroking him, and would
explain what had happened, never knowing that the
dog might have understood more than I realized.

"Dukie Boy," I would say. "Dad is on an airplane.
He's not coming back for a couple of days. He is way
up in the sky, flying. But then he will come back."

Then when we went outside together, I even would start pointing out airplanes to Duke when I saw one pass overhead. He would follow my fingers when I pointed up and explained that they were what Dad went on when he went out of town with the suitcases. I could not expect a dog to understand me, not something abstract like this, but it was as if Duke learned more than I had imagined. It was as if he made the connection between those very sad days and the tiny things in the sky.

One of Duke's favorite pastimes became lying on the deck on a clear day, with his head tilted back, watching for airplanes. Whenever he spotted one he would leap to his feet, bark like a wild animal, and run back and forth along the yard, giving chase and baying for all he was worth.

The neighbor dogs never barked with him. They just stared silently as he challenged the airplane. For all I knew, he was warning them never to take his daddy away again, and the other dogs believed he was nuts. However, Duke knew more English than I knew his barks.

Duke was a completely crazy dog, but I loved him just as crazily. Even more than the squirrels, nobody else ever figured out why he became such an anti-airplane Golden Retriever. Some people said that it was a throwback to how a Golden Retriever would have watched birds soar through the air so they could retrieve them. But Duke never cared for birds, just airplanes, so I know better. He wanted to tell those planes just how much he loved his daddy.

18 PANCAKE THE WHITE GERMAN SHEPHERD

*John, you better have those shoes off the
floor when I get in there!*

I often enjoy sitting with my 15 year old daughter and telling her stories of my childhood. Many of the stories I share with her include accounts of our family dog, Pancake. Not many memories from my early years were made without Pancake being involved. I could fill book after book with stories, but one in particular always sticks out in my memory.

Pancake was a male German Shepherd puppy, given to us by one of my father's co-workers. Pancake was born along with several siblings, and the lady who owned his mother decided she didn't want more dogs to care for. My father was a dog lover, but hadn't gotten me and my sister a dog because the home we lived in didn't allow pets. We had just moved into our own home, and I was beginning the 6th grade.

I was a 12 year old boy, full of energy and life. I will never forget the day my father walked in the door with a small box in his hands. Inside the box was a bundle of joy, a beautiful white colored puppy. Of course he was afraid, shaking and missing his mother. My sister and I began to love on him immediately. We were so excited, wrestling with each other to be the one holding him, cuddling him, and rubbing his coat. My father watched us closely, a small smile on his face. He told us to take it easy wrestling over the dog before we smashed him into a pancake. With that, the name of our dog was decided, Pancake.

As Pancake grew over the years, he became very attached to my parents, my sister, and myself. Though he slept in a dog house in the back yard, he spent most of his time with us, either inside the house or running around outside in the yard or the park across the street. My father worked really hard to get Pancake house broken, and he also worked hard to teach him numerous commands. It was very clear the dog had above average intelligence, and his ability to learn things was amazing. Pancake became a very huge part of our family. He traveled with us, attended family gatherings, and was always a presence during our family time together.

Pancake also became very protective of our family, especially my sister and I. If a stranger made a sudden move towards one of us, he would give them a precautionary growl as he slowly rose to his feet. Pancake was a friendly dog, and very obedient. Most of our neighbors and other family members knew to not make an aggressive move toward the kids.

While we were learning Pancake's personality, he was also learning ours. He knew that when my father was upset, it was best for the family to stay out of his way and allow him to rant, something he did on occasion, especially when work was extremely stressful. Pancake also knew if he didn't do his personal business outside and something was found on the floor in the house he would receive a scolding or spanking from my father.

He was such a smart dog, he learned that when my mother was cooking his favorite foods, if he just hung around the back door, eventually she would throw him something to enjoy. The level of his understanding was amazing, and people all over our neighborhood commented on it often.

The day I came to believe Pancake understood English was a Saturday. One of our family traditions was we all woke up a little late on Saturday, and then we all chipped in and cleaned the entire house. My mother constantly reminded me to pick my shoes up and place them in my closet. Usually, on Saturday I would receive a scolding from my mother because the shoes I had worn through the previous week would always be scattered on my floor. By the time I was about 16 years old, I would jump out of bed and begin to pick up my shoes, placing them in my closet in my giant shoe box. On this particular day, my mother was especially bossy, and she began to scold us for how our rooms surely looked. She was making her way through my sister's room, and I could hear her saying things like,

"John, you better have those shoes off the floor when I get in there!"

I jumped from the bed to start picking up my shoes just in time to see Pancake dropping a shoe into the box. Most of the shoes were already picked up, and he was finishing my job, just in time for my mother to enter a clean room!

I'm convinced Pancake learned over the years from hearing my mother rant about my room. On those Saturdays, he was usually perched in a corner, watching us clean. I believe he heard my mother's commands, and he understood it meant my shoes better be off the floor before she arrived.

I'm still amazed how he managed to pick each shoe up and place it where it belonged. So many things Pancake did would blow our minds, but I will always remember the day he saved me from my mother's wrath.

Pancake lived a long, healthy life. My father eventually gave him to my grandmother as she aged, so she could have some companionship and protection in her home. I went off to college, and on occasion I would venture home, always going to see Pancake. He was just as fun after I became an adult as he was when I was a young boy.

My daughter often asks me questions about my childhood, and as I happily share things from my past, we often talk about Pancake.

Whenever someone says they wonder if dogs can understand humans, I quickly answer,

"Yes, they can!"

19 RUSTY MY ENGLISH COCKER SPANIEL

I looked down at Rusty and I shouted,
"Go find Rio!"

I was walking home from my first day of school. I couldn't believe I had homework already. I just wanted to get home and see my best friend. When I reached the front stairs, Rusty my English Cocker Spaniel started barking. I opened the door and she jumped on me and licked my face because she was so happy to see me. I was so elated to see her. She really is my best friend. I had so much to do that day. I had to do my homework, practice a dance for my recital, clean my room and then take a shower. Mom was making my favorite meal because it was my first day of school. Spaghetti and meatballs, Yummy! I always share my meatballs with Rusty. She loves them.

I finished my homework and shared my spaghetti and meatballs and wanted to take a walk in the park with Rusty. Although mom told me to practice my dance first, I just couldn't wait. I wanted to go to the park with my dog. I love to spend time with her. She somehow understands me. I think she gets me more than most people.

I brought Rusty's favorite ball and I was on the swing. I was throwing the ball and she was fetching. Only this one time I threw the ball a little too far! She ran for the ball and I was looking around for a little while and I couldn't find her. I walked about a quarter mile away where the grass meets the lake. I whistled so loud for her. I heard her bark in the lake after I whistled. She knew I was calling her, although I never whistled before. I couldn't move, I was so happy she was OK and that we found each other. She safely got out of the water with the ball in her mouth. I finally could move and I ran towards Rusty. I gave her a big hug and a kiss. I was just so happy to see her again.

It was getting late and I needed to get home before my mother got worried. We ran almost all the way home because it was getting dark. As soon as I got in the door, my mom yelled "What took you so long! Practice your dance and get in the shower."

I got all my dance gear on and blasted the radio in the basement while Rusty was barking to the beat. Her favorite song is 'Who Let the Dogs Out?' which was the song I was dancing to in the recital. I dropped to the floor and Rusty came running over to hug me. I was exhausted!

I started the water for my shower, but I heard my friend outside yelling. I ran outside and Rusty followed. My friend lives next door to me. Her name is Sam and she has a parrot named Rio. She was yelling because Rio flew out of the house. I told her the story of what happened to Rusty and me that day. I tried to explain she was lost and we found each other. I told her to try calling Rio, and look in every tree and bush.

I told my mother I would be going with my friend Sam, to help her find her bird Rio. I knew how I felt that day. I couldn't think about how sad it would have been if I lost my dog. I also hated to see my friend upset. I had to do something about it.

I looked down at Rusty and I shouted,
"Go find Rio!"

Although I thought he didn't even know what that meant, all of a sudden Rusty took off on me. I couldn't believe this was happening again. I couldn't lose her. I ran after her. I could see her slowing down now. I remember thinking, "Does she see something she doesn't like, is she just tired or did she really find Rio?" I saw her going crazy and heard her barking so loud.

Sam and I ran to Rusty and she was barking at a tree.

We didn't know why she was barking at the tree. We looked and didn't see anything. We wanted to leave to look for her parrot, but Rusty would not leave the tree. I tried to take her away but she just didn't want to leave. She just sat down looking up at the tree.

I asked her, "Did you find Rio?"

The barking got so loud, and she started to scratch on the bark of the tree. It looked like she just wanted to climb up.

I thought, "Could she have understood me when I asked her to find Rio?" I didn't expect or even think she could understand me. Rusty, Sam and I sat around the tree for about an hour, and then we heard a yell from her bird.

I said, "Wow, Rio's in the tree!"

Rusty started barking again and ran around the other side of the tree. Afraid the bird wouldn't come down because of Rusty, I pulled her away back down the street to our house and watched from there.

Sam called to Rio, and eventually the bird hopped down to her. I yelled and jumped up and down in happiness. Rusty kissed me in happiness, too. I started to cry, because I was so happy. My mom came out to see what all the yelling was about and I told her the story. Rusty and I hugged so long.

I have the most amazing dog. How was it possible for Rusty to know what was going on? She knew I wanted her to find the bird.

20 GREAT DANE NAMED CHLOE

Chloe, watch Aiden.

There is no doubt in my mind that my dog understands English. I have a three year old female Great Dane named Chloe who always seems to understand what I am talking about. I got her when she was just six weeks old and we had a connection from the very start.

It all started when I went to pick out my puppy from a litter of 12. She was the runt of the litter and I really wanted her sister because she had the most beautiful markings, but I changed my mind once I met Chloe. I asked her,

"Do you want to come home with me?"

She licked my hand and laid her head down on my leg as if to say,

"Yes I would love to."

I asked all of the other puppies the same exact thing and none of them reacted this way. That was when I knew she was the one I just had to have.

We have since moved to Oregon and I feel that she is now just about the only one who really understands me. I think that had she not understood that it was going to be better in Oregon it would have made for a less pleasant trip. She was the best dog for the whole four days in the car that it took us to get out here.

Anyone will tell you their own dog understands what they say, but I'm not the only one who has said this about my dog. When she was a puppy we had her in a training class at the local pet store. The trainer even said it was like Chloe understood what we wanted her to do. She caught on to everything in the class in just minutes, unlike all of the other dogs in the class who barely had it at the end of six weeks. I am very grateful that Chloe at least seems to understand what I am telling her.

Many people are nervous when it comes to such a large dog around my newborn son, but if anything she is protective. She is great with children and she understands that he is small and that she has to be careful around him. I have seen many dogs that get jealous to the point of being violent when their owners have a new baby but it has never been that way with Chloe. There was this one time that I told her,

"Chloe, watch Aiden."

I just said it jokingly, before I took a shower. I was

more than shocked to find her lying right next to his crib when I got out. It was like she was babysitting for me while I was busy.

She will also come tell me when he starts crying. There have been several times while I've been making him a bottle that he wakes up and cries in the bedroom. She will go between the kitchen and the bedroom door like she is trying to tell me that he needs me. It really is the cutest thing ever.

She has never been all that good on a leash; she gets a little wild at first. About a week ago I had to take her to get her nails trimmed and I had to take my 2 month old son as well. I had a conversation with her before we left. I told her,

"Chloe, you have to behave a bit more than usual because it's hard for me to walk you and push the stroller at the same time."

That was the very first time that she never pulled on the leash, and there were even other dogs out. I know that she knew exactly what I told her, and that was just the last time. There have been many others.

The first time that I knew she understood for sure was when she was about a year old. She's always been allowed on our furniture and even sleeps in bed with us. We were on vacation staying with friends for a week, and they were a bit worried about having a Great Dane on their furniture, so I had a talk with her and told her,

"Chloe, while we're here, you'll have to lie on the floor."

Now, I expected to have to remind her several times because being on the bed with us was something she was just used to, but she did not even try to get on anything even once. Another time, I told Chloe,

"If you're a good girl while I'm at the store, I'll get you something while I'm there."

Now, I ended up going to a different store, and they didn't have dog treats, so I didn't get her anything. When I got home, I knew not only had she understood what I had said, she remembered. She had this look in her eyes that said,

"You said you were going to get me something."

I felt so bad that I had to go back out just to get her a treat. Now, this is not something that I do all the time, so it's not like she expected it. I had told her this time that I would, and she knew it.

I also know that she can understand how I feel most of the time. When I was pregnant with my son I was not feeling well most of the time and she was always right there by my side, even on days when I could not get out of bed, she would lie there with me the whole time. I think that having her there by my side through that time made it all go quite a bit easier than it would have been if she had not been there.

Chloe really is more than just a dog to me. She really is my best friend, especially since I am new to the area and do not have a lot of friends yet. I find myself just talking to her like she is a human when I am home alone with the baby.

21 KELLIE THE MINPIN

Kellie, go potty.

My cute little MinPin (miniature Doberman Pincher) is 5 years old and her name is Kellie. I have only had her for the last year because she belonged to my son who moved into a townhouse that doesn't accept pets. He decided to move to another state for his wife, who hadn't seen her family for the past 7 years.

My son was torn between disappointing his wife and selling Kellie until I offered to take her for him. I had just lost my Jack Russell to an accident, so he wasn't sure if I was willing to take in another dog. Needless to say, I fell in love with this little ball of energy the minute I brought her home. She is such a loving animal, and she is unbelievably perceptive.

Kellie is the type of dog who has to sleep with me in bed every night and when I say sleep with me in bed, I don't mean at the foot of the bed. I mean she has her own little pillow that she rests her head on at night and her own little blanket that she has to be covered with or she won't sleep. I can always expect to be woken by her little wet nose kisses in the morning and she has to have a really good scratching before she starts her busy day.

I've had a few dogs in my past (I am 43 years old and have had 4 dogs since my childhood), but none of them have been as smart as Kellie is. She is either very perceptive or just plain understands English, but I believe it is more of an understanding than a perception. From the day I brought Kellie home, she understood and followed basic commands. For example, I don't have the ability to take her out a lot to go to the bathroom, so I decided to lay out a puppy pad and give it a try.

I took Kellie over to the pad and told her with a firm but loving voice,

"Kellie, go potty,"

while I pointed to the pad. I did this three times throughout the morning hours when I knew she would need to go to the bathroom. After the third time, I had decided to take her out because I didn't want to have to clean up a mess. I went to grab her leash, and when I turned around, she was peeing on the pad. From that moment on, she has been pad trained.

Sure, that could be considered a coincidence or just a result of repetitive commands but there is more.

Kellie loves to take rides with me when I go out, and from the very first day, she has understood when it was time to go. All it takes is for me to say,

"Kellie, you wanna go for a ride?"

and she instantly runs over to her harness and leash and waits for me to put them on her. She will not move until she is strapped up and ready to go.

When I open the front door, she will run to her car door (which is where her little doggy car seat is set up) and wait for me to open it. When I do get it open, she jumps into the car and right up into her doggy car seat waiting to be fastened in. These are all just pieces of a line of things that I know Kellie understands. She isn't simply listening to sounds and perceiving what they mean. I believe she truly understands what I say when I talk to her.

Kellie is a very obedient dog and she has been from day one. I love to eat grapes and strawberries and now Kellie does too. She took notice the first time I walked to my little room refrigerator where I keep snacks I want quick access to. After giving her the first grape she ever ate, she fell in love with them. Now, all I have to say is,

"You want a grapie?"

and she literally bolts to the refrigerator. But if I say the word 'grapie', I better go over and get her one or I'm in the dog house.

I can't say for sure whether or not these are simple coincidence or if Kellie actually understands the words that I am saying, but I know this for sure: all it takes for Kellie to remember and follow an instruction is to be told it once. I think that the original example of the puppy pad took Kellie three times because she didn't have to go to the potty at that particular time. If she had, she probably would have done it right away. This is the impression I get every time she follows a different set of instructions.

As I stated earlier, Kellie is a very obedient dog and that isn't because my son taught her any of the things she does here with me. I've already asked him if he used puppy pads, a car seat for dogs, or let her eat grapes and he said not a chance. This only confirms my belief that Kellie understands what I say.

I will actually sit with her and hold a conversation (which would probably land me in the psych ward) watching the expressions on her cute little face. I believe that if she could only vocalize what she was thinking, she would have a lot to say.

My dog Kellie is the most intelligent dog I have ever had the privilege of owning and I do truly believe that she understands English.

[Cherise's note: The first time Kellie responded to an English word, when she peed on the pad after being told to "go potty," impresses me because she hadn't been taught that. This reminds me of when an older historian from England corrected us when we told our dog to "go potty." She said, "It makes no sense, telling an animal that." When I looked at her in confusion, she explained, "Don't you know where that saying comes from?" I shook my head. "It's from the chamber pots people used to keep inside so that they didn't have to go use the outdoor facility, back before plumbing. Why you'd tell a dog to use one is beyond me." I explained it's what we tell toddlers and so it just comes out of our mouths naturally when we command dogs. Then it was her turn to look confused, heh!]

22 BUSTER, A CHIHUAHUA AND DACHSHUND MIX

Not yet, Buster. You've gotta wait a little bit before you can eat.

I'm here to let you know about my dog, Buster, and how he has grown to become a part of my family.

Ever since I met my dog, I've felt that he sometimes understands what my family or I are trying to communicate with him. He first appeared at our doorstep about 10 years ago. He's a Chihuahua and Dachshund mix, and is absolutely a joy to have around the house, and although it's taken some years to properly train and teach him simple commands as far as taking care of his business outdoors, there are no headaches or hassles involved with having him around the house.

In fact, even with Buster being our first and only dog we've ever had, we cannot imagine a home without a dog.

We decided to name our new found dog Buster.

The first day he appeared at our door, my sister and I nearly begged our parents to allow us to keep him. We'd never thought about getting ourselves a dog, but realized that it must have been a sign or calling for us to allow him to live with us. I mean, he basically came and knocked on our door, without actually knocking.

If I recall correctly, he was sitting around our porch for some time before he got brave and came up to the door. He was such a little puppy at the time, maybe around 1 or 2 months old at the most. Since it was a surprise appearance, we obviously had no dog food prepared for him. So we decided to give him some edibles that were for us. We fed him a sliced up hot dog, a little bit of bread and lots of water in case he was dehydrated. Buster very much enjoyed the food. I think we named him Buster after a cartoon character from a TV show my sister and I used to watch regularly.

After some years of training Buster, he has learned to be very polite. When we grab his food from the fridge or pantry, he almost always realizes that he's about to be fed and quietly sits calmly either under the dinner table or by the counter to wait for us to serve it in his food bowl. However, sometimes I feel that he understands what we are saying. Oftentimes, we may say something like

"Buster, are you ready to eat?"

and he'll get a little jumpy and head towards the kitchen area. This is incredible as it shows his understanding and intelligence. Sometimes, we'll tell Buster,

"Not yet, Buster. You've gotta wait a little bit before you can eat."

and he goes away and sits back in the living room because he understands what we're telling him!

It is very strange because it feels as if we're able to talk to him.

Buster has been very good about waiting until we open the door for him to go outside and take care of business. Even if it means waiting for many hours during the day. We don't make him wait for long on purpose. That would be similar to cruel punishment. However, when my family or I are at school or work, it's not possible to let him out. Also, we don't like to let him stay outside for too long because he's small and if it gets too hot outside he may not be able to handle the heat. Therefore, we keep him inside for comfort and relaxing. There have been some instances where Buster has proven to us that he's not human and leaked on the carpet in some places. He's only a dog, so it's forgivable each time. However, I'm very proud to say that we hardly ever have a problem with him going in the house.

As I've made clear, sometimes it seems like Buster truly understands English. When my dad goes out for his morning walks, he will usually take Buster along without a leash. Buster likes to walk around freely, but as soon as my dad realizes he's about to handle his business on someone else's lawn, my dad will shout,

"No, Buster!"

and Buster will happily walk away as soon as he hears the command. Then, he will wait until he reaches our own yard to use the bathroom. We've become lenient on Buster though, and allow him to urinate in open parks and fields, and always pick up after his bowel movements to keep up with the city's rules and regulations for pet walking.

As soon as Buster gets home from a long walk, he heads right for the water bowl in which he will indulge nearly a whole bowl full. Then, just for his reaction's sake, we will ask him,

"Buster, are you ready to eat?"

and he will almost always go and wait where he normally does when we take out his food. He must understand what we are asking him because he almost always performs the same actions.

We hate to see Buster looking as if he is sad. For as long as we've had him and how well trained he has become, he's basically a part of the family. However, we feel like Buster has such good manners that our training may have had nothing to do with his ways. He may just be a good dog that may not have required any training to begin with. We greatly appreciate our dog and would not trade him for anything else in this world. If anyone decides to keep a dog for the long term, they must realize that they will grow to love him no matter what.

23 MAYHEM AND CHAOS THE MUTTS

Is that what you really want to do? Chew on your blanket?

I am the proud owner of two mutts. And I say that with as much love as possible. Well, they are not really mutts. My two pups are actually Labrador Retriever mixes, and they are brothers from the same litter. The mother was a Lab, and the father was an English Pointer. We were not exactly sure of the father's breed, at first, because we adopted them from a rescue, just last year. As the pups got older, we started to figure out their father's breed. One of them, Mayhem, had the spots of a Pointer since he was a puppy, but we were not completely sure that was what he was until he started pointing at birds, squirrels and the like.

We had searched high and low for the one perfect puppy ... but we came home with two. In fact, my husband and I had discussed, that very morning, the idea of two, and had decided there was no way. One puppy would be enough work. We could not handle two. So how is it possible that we did, in fact, come home with two? Well, it is simple, really. We had scoured the rescue websites and found Chaos, our little black and white puppy. We chatted with the lady who owned the rescue. Chaos had four brothers, and all five puppies would be at an adoption event that Saturday.

We headed out early. Even though we had already told her we wanted him, filled out our application, and been approved, we didn't want anyone else to try and adopt our little guy.

We got there, and there were the five puppies. One came right over to me, a gorgeous white, gray and black spotted pup. I picked him up and he nuzzled right into me. I turned around and said, "Can I have him? I promise I can handle two!" My husband said he had no choice. My big eyes and that cute puppy won him over in a heartbeat. So, we came home with two.

It's true that two puppies are a lot of work. There were times when I cried. Potty training two? Holy cow what a job. But they are so worth it. I love that they each have a playmate in the other and are never bored.

As to their names, yes, one of the dogs is named Chaos. The other we named Mayhem. Yes, I know, and yes, they live up to their names. One is always causing trouble, and the other seems to just go along, and it's never the same dog making the trouble. They seem to swap up days. "You be bad today. It's your turn. I'll be bad tomorrow," they seem to say to one another. And they are not really 'bad', just mischievous and full of energy. The two boys are just a year old, and are still very much puppies in nature.

Chaos and Mayhem wrestle, run around, fight (good naturedly) over toys … and they love to play tug of war. One day when Chaos was chewing on a bone, Mayhem decided, of course, that the bone was the exact thing he wanted to chew on, too. Now this is not surprising. This is what they do every single day. One guy picks one toy or bone to chew on, and then the other guy tries to take it away from him. They actually seem to love this game.

This particular day had Mayhem winning and stealing the bone away from Chaos. So, Chaos did what any self-respecting pup would do: he pouted. He left the play area and went into his crate (or as we call them, "the box").

I laughed and then went over to comfort poor Chaos. As I was talking to him, he started to chew on the blanket in his crate, because he was so mad. I asked him,

"Is that what you really want to do? Chew on your blanket?"

After I said this, Mayhem got up off the rug, stopped chewing on his bone and came over, grabbed Chaos's blanket and began pulling, trying to get his brother to play tug of war.

Now, our dogs have been through puppy training and they graduated. They know basic commands such as 'sit', 'stay', 'down' and 'paw.' They have also learned a great deal of 'fun' language, as I like to call it.

They know 'walk', 'peanut butter', 'Kongs' (a doggy toy that you fill with peanut butter and we use as a crate treat), 'daycare' (doggy daycare, which they get to go to once a week, and they love), and 'park', which is the dog park that we go to quite frequently.

But one word I've never taught them is 'blanket'. Mayhem couldn't see us from his view point, but as soon as I mentioned that Chaos was chewing on his blanket, Mayhem was up off the floor, heading to Chaos's crate, and then tugging Chaos's blanket away from him. I couldn't believe it!

That night I told my husband the story. I told him I was positive that our dogs understood English, but seemed to have selective hearing. They only choose to follow the commands they want, when they think it will get them a treat.

[Cherise's note: A child psychologist and I were discussing our dogs once, the way other people discuss their children. She says a dog psychologist told her that dogs have IQs of about 70, which is the low end of the human IQ spectrum. She said he also told her the average dog knows more than 200 words. I was suitably impressed, but then we started talking about our dogs' favorite words, just like people talk about their kids' favorite words. I told her our dogs' favorite words are 'food', 'park', 'walk', 'treat', 'outside', 'dogs', and 'yeah' (because it means yeah, they get to come along). Unfortunately, one of our dogs could hear me. He was overly excited for the next few minutes, wagging his tail and jumping around. Poor guy.]

24 TRUMAN THE SHIH TZU

Do you feel lucky?

Getting over the unexpected loss of my husband when he was only 45 was very difficult, and my own health deteriorated as I became a shut in, meaning I never left the house. I sought professional help, and the therapist that I was regularly going to used dogs as a form of therapy, pet therapy she called it. She had a breeder that specially bred dogs to act as service dogs, or perform other tasks, or just give comfort to their human companions.

I connected with this breeder and told her that I didn't have a huge amount of preferences for this dog, but I would like a male, and she said she had one male left from her current liter. I told her I would take him sight unseen, as I was a shut in. She brought him over.

He was just shy of 4 months old. I already knew I would call him Truman after the writer that always inspired me. The breeder Randy arrived at my home, with her dad in tow, and a pet carrier. She took Truman out of the carrier and there was this 5 pound black and white little fur ball. He was just adorable. He had the biggest dark brown eyes I ever saw. He is a full bred Shih Tzu. He looked a lot like Obie, our old dog, and in the beginning I would forget and sometimes call him Obie.

While Truman was sniffing around on the carpet, I asked Randy the breeder, "So when is his birthday?" She said, "March 23." I nearly fell down with that revelation. I asked Randy, "Really?" She replied, "Yes, Really." March 23 was my late husband's birthday. There were some strange coincidences that were adding up.

We did have to work together, Randy and me, for Truman's training, and we did that for a few months, a few days a week. However, I was very quickly learning how very special my sweet little boy was and is. He's extremely smart, and I felt an instant connection to this little fella.

He would look at me with his big brown eyes and just know what I was feeling or thinking. It was truly amazing. I was starting to feel that perhaps my husband was with me again, that he had come back as Truman.

The theory on this type of therapy is that people with grave anxiety issues, like myself, concentrate on the welfare of the dog instead of what makes them anxious. As far as my own mental health, having Truman has repaired my health. I'm no longer a shut in, and I'm living life again. I don't think this would be the case without my little Truman. He's truly a miracle, and I feel very lucky that we were able to find each other. We are always together, never apart.

I just have to say things once, and he just knows. Whether we have learned something or not, he always knows. If I say,

"Go on the couch,"

he jumps on it. During the day, he's with me in my small tiny office, and I do mean tiny. So often times I have to tell him either to jump on or jump off a Futon I have in the office. When we visit my Mom who lives nearby, I say to him,

"We're going to see Nana now,"

and he starts jumping all over the place. That is something we never practiced, he just picked it up immediately.

He knows things we never worked on. He understands me better than any person that is currently in my life. He teaches me about life every single day. He guides me through this world, with no motives other than to be there for me. He's hands down my very best friend. He never judges me. He's always happy. He is the happiest little fella that I have ever known. I feel so lucky and truly blessed that a little 10 pounds of goodness is in my life. He doesn't have a mean bone in his body. He's a true extrovert. He always wants to see and talk to everyone he sees, people and other dogs.

He is smarter than most people. I feel like with Truman in my corner, anything is possible. He also understands

"Do you feel lucky?"

He knows what that means. I will ask him if he feels lucky, and if he reacts to that question, I buy a lottery ticket.

Every single time I've bought a ticket based on his reaction, I have won. Anywhere from 1 dollar to 300 dollars. It's truly amazing.

He's an amazing gift, and I'm grateful that he and I were able to find each other. Everyone should be lucky enough to have a Truman in their life. My life has been truly enriched because he is in it. He's made me a better person, and a functioning person, in that I'm no longer a shut in. I tell everyone that he's given me my life back, and I don't take that for granted. I'm thinking of learning Chinese. I'm sure if we learned together, he would be able to understand that language too.

25 PADDY, A GREYHOUND/ BORDER COLLIE MIX

I need my medicine.

In January of 2012, we had just moved into our brand new house. I had just entered my second trimester. We were pregnant with our first child. My husband had just been hired on at a really great company. Life was going pretty good for us, and we wanted to expand our little family further.

We decided it was time to adopt a playmate for our miniature schnauzer puppy, Bob. We also decided the next dog needed to be a larger breed because my husband wanted a dog he could exercise with. While my husband was at work one evening he saw a flyer advertising puppies in need of permanent homes. These puppies had been in foster homes through Faithful Friends Animal Advocates out of Neosho, Missouri. My husband soon found out that the foster home had two puppies available, a boy and girl named Paddy and Paxton. We were initially told they were Border Collie / Black Lab mix puppies.

One weekend we drove to Neosho to meet these puppies. The foster family encouraged us to bring Bob to play with them. They brought in Paddy first. From the very first moment, Bob and Paddy hit it off. They played so well together that we knew she was the perfect match for our family. Before we decided to permanently adopt Paddy, we visited another humane society but no other dog seemed to get along with Bob. After leaving the shelter, we knew Paddy was our dog. We called the foster family and scheduled our adoption date.

At first I felt guilty taking her away from the only home she knew. Paddy was a small puppy when her mother was left alone with her eight puppies tied to a tree. A member of Faithful Friends Animal Advocates found her mom and the puppies and took them in. A few days later they were placed with a foster family. When we brought Paddy home she was eight months old. As Paddy got older she looked less like a Black Lab and more like a Greyhound. We firmly believe she's a Greyhound / Border Collie mix.

[Cherise's note: That's part of the fun of rescuing dogs from the animal shelter. You get to play the game of guessing which breeds they're a mix of. ☺]

A few months after adopting Paddy, I started getting this horrible pain in the right side of my abdomen. The pain didn't get any better. One night my husband took me to the emergency room. Our biggest fear was that I might be going into pre-term labor. When we got to the emergency room I was told to go straight to the maternity ward. After numerous tests it was determined to be round ligament pain. I can remember doubting it was round ligament pain.

Within the next few weeks I was hospitalized for what they believed was appendicitis. After several more tests I was diagnosed with biliary dyskinesia. This is a disease involving the gallbladder. I was past the point of safely removing my gallbladder.

The doctor decided my treatment options would be hydrocodone around the clock. There was no way I was okay with taking pain medicine of that strength while being pregnant. The doctor explained to me that having high blood pressure from being in pain all the time was more dangerous than taking the medicine. I decided at that point I would only take the medicine if the pain got unmanageable.

One afternoon while my husband was at work Paddy came and rested her head on my lap. I was into my third trimester and around 30 weeks. I kept telling Paddy to go lie down but no matter what I did she wouldn't listen. I found this to be odd because she usually listens.

Within 10 minutes, I had the worst gallbladder attack of all time.

Sometimes gallbladder attacks stop quickly, and other times they can drag out for hours. I remember lying on the bathroom floor in so much pain. Paddy sat next to me the entire time. I finally got to the point where I wanted to go lie down on the couch, but being in pain and pregnant, getting off the floor wasn't an easy task.

She allowed me to use her as a balance to get up. Once I was on the couch, I realized I needed to take the medicine. I remember saying out loud,

"I need my medicine."

It was on my husband's desk next to the Tylenol and Aspirin. Paddy got off the couch and went over to the desk and brought me my prescription bottle.

That was the first time she had ever done that, and from that point on whenever she sensed I was fixing to have another attack she would bring me my pill bottle.

The gallbladder attacks didn't last the remaining time of my pregnancy. By the time I hit 33 weeks, they eased up and I was able to completely stop taking the medicine. A few months after our son was born, I began having gallbladder issues again. At this point it was determined I needed surgery.

Paddy has always had such a nurturing sense about her. From the first day we brought her home she was always the first one to lie down and cuddle close. She gets along with everyone she meets. She loves cats and other dogs. Sometimes she's been known to get over excited and hyper, but that's because she's a mix between two high energy breeds. She requires a lot of exercise. She does great on the leash and off the leash. Paddy is now my 13 month old baby's best friend.

She still dashes to my side whenever I get sick.

26 NIKKI THE GOLDEN GERMAN SHEPHERD

You go in the living room and sit down
until I get in to speak with you.

I once had a golden German Shepherd whose name was Nikki. I had rescued her and it seemed she always knew that I had saved her. She was a bright and funny dog that seemed to know more than I would give her credit for. She was tolerant of children playing excessively around her and with her. She even tolerated when a younger child tried to ride on her back. She had a calm well-mannered disposition, but she always let people know if she didn't trust them. Most often she would simply give a light nip at the back of their feet to give them a warning sign that she was watching them and she didn't trust them.

Like most loyal German Shepherds she followed commands rather well. She had gone to puppy training and knew the common commands of 'sit', 'stay', 'speak', 'catch', 'fetch', and 'tag'. But she also seemed to know so much more than that at times. Most dogs know the terms: 'go for a walk', 'bye, bye car', 'go for a ride', 'want a biscuit?', 'where's the bone?', 'good', 'bad', and of course 'speak'. But she also had the most uncanny way of knowing other words on occasions that always left me wondering if she was part human. Sometimes I pondered how she could understand and know words that were rarely used around the house, never mind words I never used in a command to her.

Some of the peripheral words and phrases I used that caught her attention were: 'yard', 'go for a swim', 'ice cream', 'toy', 'cold outside', and 'sing'. Yes, in fact there were a few occasions when I would talk about singing when she would chime in with a 'roooo' or two.

They say German Shepherds have an incredible level of intelligence for a dog. That is why they are used for police dogs and rescue dogs. We lived on a lake, my daughter and I, and she played guard dog for many years. She had no problem vocally letting people know she was around on occasion. But to me I must say when she would sing out a 'roooo' or two when I would so much as mention the word sing. I would get a great chuckle.

Sometimes we would just sing together all three of us. It was quite funny! I would start a song, a fun melodic song like Do-Re-Me from the Sound of Music, and of course it was easy for my daughter to sing right along, but before you knew it, Nikki was singing alongside us trying to keep harmony.

She was a rising star and seemed to know her talent amazed me. While many dogs get singing when triggered by a specific pitch or sound, Nikki loved all singing and could chime in at the most unexpected songs and sounds, including commercials that had singing jingles in them. This was long before people posted videos online. In fact, the Internet was scarcely known by people except in the world of business. But I have no doubt her repertoire would have gone viral had people witnessed her infamous singing ability.

Of all the times she amazed me, I think the one that truly stunned me the most was the day I was angry at her for digging a hole in the yard. I knew she was simply doing what dogs do, and she loved the cooler ground that she could get to by digging and it had been warmer than usual outside. Living on a lake allows for a great breeze that can cool things down quite a bit in contrast to the other towns nearby. But it still had been a particularly warm summer. But I had just covered the area she dug up and scolded her a few days before and put plantings there to deter her from digging. I put her runner out near the big shaded tree in the back yard, and she had cleared away every blade of grass in that area and dug a cool spot for herself there as well.

But on this day, when I saw that she had dug a "hole to China" in the very spot I had planted new flowers, I got angry and scolded her in a way that was more like yelling at my young daughter at the time.

I said,

"Bad Nikki, no dig! You go in the living room and sit down until I get in to speak with you."

Seconds after I said it, I realized that I was speaking to her like I would scold my daughter. But much to my amazement, she did exactly as I had asked her to do.

She got up out of the dug hole, walked in through the sliding door through the kitchen into the living room, and sat down and waited for me.

I could scarcely believe my eyes. I could not help but chuckle as I followed a minute behind her. In fact, she stayed in that very spot until I was done patching up the hole she had dug and I had salvaged a few flowers to replant there.

I finally realized I had to shorten her runner in order to stop her from digging, so that she couldn't reach the side of the house. But her uncanny ability to know human words that I would say to my daughter never ceased to make me smile, and never ceased to amaze me.

27 YULA MY JACK RUSSELL TERRIER

Yula, go get help. Go get Mom.

Being a shy child, I didn't make that many friends, as no one wants to talk to the shy boy.

A few days before Christmas when I was six, I was sitting on the floor watching TV. My dad placed a white box in front of me, tied up with a blue ribbon, and then sat down on the couch with Mom. I looked up at him with confusion on my face. I remember thinking, 'What is this for? Christmas is still a few days away. Why is he giving me a gift now?'

"Open it, then." He eagerly said with a slight grin on his face. Mom said nothing but just watched, trying to conceal her excitement.

I looked the box over before carefully raising my hand to the end of the bow, taking hold of the end and tugging at it to loosen it till it fell off.

The lid began to move by itself, making me jump back a little. That was odd, I thought to myself. I moved closer toward the box, slowly lifting the lid to peer inside. A black nose poked out, along with a tiny wet tongue, licking the air. Realizing it was the pup I had been admiring for what seemed a long time now, my heart pounded with excitement. I reached into the box and pulled her out. Her little tail wagged excitedly as if she knew she would someday be mine.

From that day forward, Yula and I had a connection that only two best friends can have. She understood basic commands such as 'sit' and 'stay', but I wanted so much more than that. I wanted her to understand me and even to talk back to me. I know that sounds crazy. Dogs don't talk, let alone understand humans. But she was my best friend and she knew every secret of mine.

As time went by, things began to change for Yula and me. Never was there a time when we were apart, but she began to show me things I have never seen in a dog. It started off with me saying little things such as,

"Go get your Frisbee out of your toy box," or "Go get your teddy pig,"

and she would. This stirred an excitement within me. Was she beginning to understand me?

I put her to the test, pushing her further to see if she indeed understood my every word. I would tell her, as I would a friend, that I was going for a walk and would she like to come with me. Her excitement could not be concealed, her tail and body shaking wildly until I got her leash and headed out the door.

"Yula, I'm going to go play in the yard, would you

like to join me?"

Again she would show the excitement in her body and she'd head for the back door.

Yula would listen to me when I felt sad or alone. I would tell her about my day at school. If I had a bad day she would sit at the end of my bed with me, sadness in her eyes as if she was feeling the same as I. She would lick my cheek as if to console me, to try and cheer my heart once more. She would feel my joy on good days and her tail would wag along with my joy.

This brought joy to my heart and a new excitement to my life. I felt as if I had found a true friend, someone who would listen to me, and even though she could not reply back to me, she would show me her love in her actions.

One day, I decided to go on an adventure. So off I went with my best friend Yula. We went down to the shed down the back of the yard. Mom didn't like me going down there as it was dangerous. The lock had become rusted and at times would lock itself. I felt adventurous today and wanted to see what was inside the mysterious shed.

"Mom, we're going to play in the yard,"

I called out as we headed out the door. We ran as fast as we could towards the shed before mom could say anything more. I managed to easily undo the lock and we snuck inside. The door closed behind us, leaving us in pitch darkness except for a small leak of light from a hole in the side of the shed. The shed was very eerie. I couldn't see a thing except Yula.

"OK, this wasn't as much fun as I thought it would be,"

I told her. I tried to open the door but it was locked. I began to panic and started to beat on the door, screaming out for Mom. She couldn't hear me. She was too far away in the house. I started to cry, believing we would be trapped forever in the shed.

Yula started to pine along with me, so for her I regained my strength and tried to sooth her, whilst figuring a way out. My attention was drawn to the light peering through the hole. She would be small enough to fit, right?

"Yula, go get help. Go get Mom,"

I pleaded with her. I could see a glint in her eye. I knew she was listening. Yula made her way to the hole and squeezed herself through with little effort. Next, she was gone. Fear struck my heart again as now I was alone in this darkness. After what seemed to be forever, I heard Mom calling my name.

"Mike? Are you in there?"

The shed door unlocked and the light beamed in. I threw my arms around Mom, holding her tight to me, sobbing and thanking her for rescuing me. Mom told me that Yula was the true hero as she was the one who came to her, barking until Mom followed her to the shed.

I have never yet met another dog like Yula. She really was one special Jack Russell.

28 A SIBERIAN HUSKY NAMED MAYA

Maya, if you don't get in this house right NOW, when I catch you, I am taking you to the pound myself!

My husband and I adopted a Siberian Husky named Maya. Maya was 14 months old when she came to live with us. She has the most beautiful crystal blue eyes and she genuinely smiles. She was beyond hyper when we adopted her, and her favorite thing to do was bolt out the door if left unattended.

When that happened, she would dance around just out of arm's reach, daring you to chase her. Just an FYI, it does NO good to chase a Siberian Husky. They are fast, much faster than humans. Any and all efforts to prove that point wrong are futile. Your best bet is to wait until she gets tired, offer her a treat, and watch her trot into the house with that face full of a smile that says,

"Thanks for the jog. I needed that!"

Needless to say, our first few months with Maya were filled with the word 'no'.

"No, Maya! Off the couch!"

"No, Maya! Off the bed!"

"No, Maya! The cat is not a squeaky toy!"

It was like we had a toddler in the house again. Little did I know, the entire time we were speaking to her and trying to get her to understand the basics of being a good dog, she was laughing at us. Things would go like this:

"Down, Maya."

This command would be followed by a dramatic flop and a tremendous grin.

We would coo a "Good Girl!" and turn our backs while she jumped in the air and landed on her feet. And the process would begin again.

"Down, Maya!"

Flop, grin, coo, turn, jump.

It was a never ending battle. All this time, she knew what she was doing and was playing with us.

Don't be led to believe we are horribly strict masters. We love our animals with all our hearts. We give then treats, play with them, and roll around on the floor with them and make complete fools of ourselves in the process. But by the same token, we don't like rolling over on our pillow to a face-full of fur. They are more than welcome to shed on the floor to their heart's content. They can chew on their toys until they are in shreds. But the toilet bowl will always be off limits, as well as my favorite shoes.

Time goes by and we have had Maya for about a year. We are still struggling with some of the same issues day after day to have Maya become our good girl. She has put on weight and looks much healthier. Her coat is now shiny and thick, and she has calmed down and is no longer afraid of her shadow. She still thinks our bed is more comfortable than hers, loves the toilet brush as a chew toy, and is dying to see what the cat tastes like, but in most aspects, she has come a long way. She has in almost every way except her bolting. I was frustrated beyond frustration and I had to research it.

Guess what?

Huskies are known for being super smart and super stubborn (ya think?), for sneaking, and for bolting. How to break them from it? Not much hope for us there, especially since we hadn't raised her from a puppy.

I was at my wit's end. All of this time I knew she understood me. I knew she understood right from wrong, that she was happy with us, and that even so she was going to continue to scoot out the door every opportunity she had. The hubby and I were so worried she was going to get hurt. I was worried she would get picked up and sent to the pound. We had even followed her in the minivan a time or two. (Did you know Huskies can run almost 45 miles an hour?) She had gotten out onto the main road, and we were driving about that fast and she was keeping up with us. The neighbors were also getting angry because she would get their dogs all wound up. They had threatened to call the dog catchers. I was beside myself.

Fast forward to the day I came to realize that my dog understood English. No joke, she has understood every word I have told her since the day she came to live with me. I am convinced of it!

I had just gotten home from the longest day of running errands. I had armloads of groceries and bags to carry in. The hubby wasn't home to help, and the kids were at school. It was raining like crazy and I was tracking mud everywhere. One of the bags I was carrying contained a dozen eggs. It was slipping from my hand.

I broke concentration for that split second to save the eggs, and like a flash, Maya was out the front door and dancing in the rain. I literally screamed my frustration. I was exhausted; I did not have the energy to deal with her or the neighbors when they discovered she was out again. I stomped out onto the porch, hands on my hips in the pouring rain, stared at my wayward dog with flames shooting out of my eyes and smoke coming out of my ears. I mentally dared her to run. My words went something like this, through gritted teeth because I was seething!

"Maya, if you don't get in this house right NOW, when I catch you, I am taking you to the pound myself!"

What happened next was a miracle. She stopped dancing, quit grinning, put her tail between her legs, and slowly made her way to the front door. She licked my hand, walked right in and waited for me just inside.

I KNEW dogs understood English, and I have never had to threaten her with doggie jail again!

29 A DACHSHUND NAMED LEE

Who's at the door? Is it Pop?

I live in a small town, and I want to tell you about a very special little dog, my family's four legged little sweetheart. We have a seven-year-old female Dachshund named Lee. Lee is a tan Dachshund with black stripes. She has the cutest little waddle you would ever want to see. When she stretches out across the floor with her hind legs behind her, she looks like a baby seal. It is so cute. We call her Tink because when she walks, her claws make a 'tink, tink, tink' sound on our hardwood floors. We got her from a wonderful lady who rescues dogs. Dogs are a great way to help children learn responsibility. Although we got her for my son, she is definitely a family pet. She gets and gives lots of love to every member of my family.

Lee is a happy dog. It looks like she is smiling all the time. She is an amazing little dog. Sometimes it seems like she is almost human. She is very jealous. She doesn't like it when I pay attention to anyone but her. She will push her way in between me and whomever I am with. She makes strange sounds like she is trying to talk.

If I say, "I love you," then Lee will make moaning sounds back to me. It's almost like she is trying to say, "I love you too."

Like all dogs, Lee understands when asked if she has to go outside. She will run over to where I keep the leash and wait for me to put it on her. Then, she runs to the door and waits for me to open it. Once the door is open, she runs outside to do her things. But Lee seems to understand so much more than just "Do you have to go out?"

Lee's favorite food is chicken. Chicken is the first treat my family gave her. When you ask her if she wants chicken her ears perk up and her eyes widen. It's like she is listening to hear someone open the refrigerator door and get her some chicken. When you offer her some chicken, she does her famous 'tick pretty Lee', which is what my family calls it when she stands up on her hind legs. It's amazing that a little dog can even do that. Lee will stand on her hind legs and almost dance if you are holding a piece of chicken in front of her.

Like all dogs, Lee is a pack animal. We, her human family, are her pack. She knows each one of our names and who is coming when that name is said. If for example you tell her,

"Daddy's home!"

then her ears perk up and she listens for the door to open so she can greet my husband as he comes through the door.

Lee loves to be talked to. The way she moves her head and the sounds that she makes when someone is talking to her make people wonder if she does understand what is being said to her. If you say,

"Kisses!"

then Lee will kiss you and turn her head so you can kiss her back. If you don't kiss her, she will bark like she is mad because you didn't kiss her back. If you do kiss her, she will kiss you again. This can go back and forth for a long time. It usually doesn't stop until the human who is kissing her stops. If she hasn't had enough kisses, then she will bark at you and turn her cheek when you look at her to see what she's barking about.

Lee is so funny if someone knocks at the door. She runs to the door, looks at it and waits. If you ask her,

"Who's at the door? Is it Pop?"

Then she shakes her head 'no' if it's not him or 'yes' if it is him. She must know who it is by the way they knock on the door or something. When you ask her who is at the door, it looks like she's shaking her head yes or no. If it's someone we know and we ask the right name, then she always gets it right.

[Cherise's note: I'm sure Lee can smell who it is. Every source I checked said dogs can smell things outside for up to a mile away, so I'm sure Lee can smell people outside through the crack under the front door. Still, isn't it adorable to think of Lee shaking her head yes or no as her humans name all the people who might be there? ☺]

If you hold a piece of cheese in one hand and a hot dog in the other and ask Lee if she wants cheese or a hot dog she will point to what she wants. Or, she will walk over and touch your hand with her nose, letting you know which she would like to eat.

Lee is very bright. She has a lot of toys to keep her busy. If you ask her to bring you her hotdog, she can find it in a group of toys. How does she know which toy we're asking for? She must be smart. Can all dogs do this trick? Lee also understands when you tell her,

"It's time to go to bed."

She will run into the bedroom and jump up onto the bed. That is where she sleeps, at the end of my bed, by my feet. Sometimes, she'll tell me it's time to go to bed. She will jump on the bed and start barking because I'm not in there with her.

I hope everyone has a wonderful pet like my little girl Lee. She's a dog, but she thinks she's a human. She tries to talk to us. It is like she understands what we're saying to her. She is very smart and always knows what she wants. Lee is the greatest dog I've ever had.

30 RUSTY THE POMERANIAN

Time for bed.

I have a male Pomeranian that is about seven years old. He has a reddish color coat and goes by no other name than that which fits, Rusty. He likes to be the center of attention and loves belly rubs at all hours of the day. The first time I met this little guy was in August four years ago. A friend's daughter and her fiancé lived in a one bedroom apartment. The week they were finalizing wedding plans they needed to have a person to doggy sit. At first I was only supposed to watch him for the week of the wedding and the two weeks afterwards while the newlyweds were on their honeymoon. When the couple returned from their honeymoon the landlord of the apartment told them they could not keep the dog.

I brought the little guy Rusty home to meet the rest of the family. He was so cute with his big brown eyes, wet black nose and bushy tail. Immediately I began to bond with him. I would let him sit next to me while watching television. He is my best friend and part of the family. I find that there are times when we are taking our afternoon walk that he is alert to his surroundings. His little ears are perked up to listen to my voice or nature. I've found that I would rather talk to him than to the other adults in the house.

When we are getting ready to go outside or in the car I use a vocabulary similar to what I used with my children when they were pre-school age. I've found when I say,

"Let's go bye-bye" or "Let's go potty,"

he gets excited and wags his tail. I believe he understands that I am talking to him because of the pitch and tone used in my voice.

When other people in the family try to say the same sentence or similar, he will just look up at them and wag his tail. I do spoil him with giving him a favorite doggy treat that I buy at a specialty store that make doggy cookies with icing…

I have learned to be patient with him when he has an anxiety problem. He shows me unconditional love, and in return I make sure that he gets the right healthy food, plenty of water, and a place he can feel safe. He helps me take care of exercising to keep both of us fit along with staying healthy.

I believe all animals have a way to understand languages verbally but also by body language. Domestic pets like dogs or cats not only understand the language of their owners but have unique dispositions with emotion.

Rusty and I are pals. He shows me he's listening by

perking his ears up while I'm talking. There are times during the hot summer days where we enjoy the above ground pool in our back yard. Last year I went online and bought a floating device and a cabana to protect him from the summer heat. He doesn't like puddles from rain or thunderstorms and he doesn't like getting his paws wet. He has his own clothes, a rain slicker for spring rains and a parka for the cold Midwest winter months. Now that football season is here, we will both put our team jerseys on and watch Sunday football.

During the evening walks I take him on a prairie path where he sniffs out bunnies and chases them into the tall grass. He tries to hop like the bunnies he is trying to catch and never seems to catch them. I call his name and he comes without any arguments. I feel that at times he listens better than anyone else in my house.

Rusty smiles when you tickle him behind his back leg. He is a true friend and better behaved than children. He enjoys our companionship by cuddling next to me. When I say,

"Time for bed,"

he jumps on the bed between the pillows. If my wife isn't home, then he will lay his head on the pillow.

When he speaks he tells me it is time to play or he puts a paw on my hand to let me know that it is our time. He has been there for me as I go through a healing process from surgery that I had earlier this year. We communicate just like an infant does with any parent who bonds with a child.

Rusty understands me and I understand what he needs. We communicate in the English language and body language. He has picked me to be his owner, although at times he plays with the female cat of the house. Her name is Patches.

Day or night, he is usually at my side or by my feet while I am working from home.

Rusty and I enjoy the four seasons, especially when we go for our walks in the local state parks. He enjoys playing in the leaves that have fallen from the trees. Rusty might not understand the concept of space or time because of the dog brain, but he does know what it feels like to be safe, and loved by me.

[Cherise's note: I know, this story really isn't about the dog obeying an unusual command he wasn't taught. But it is about the dog and the human getting along in perfect harmony. I love how he says he would rather talk to his dog than most people, and how he says the dog is always with him wherever he goes in the house. Our dogs both follow me around the house. I'm the one who's home all the time because I work from home, too. I take both of them for their walk most days. Most days I'm the one who feeds them both. When my husband is home, he has me hand Raffle his food so that my husband can be the one who feeds Raffle, but I think Raffle knows it's really me who feeds him and that's why he follows me around. They're both lying by my feet even right now as I type this while my husband sleeps in the other room. They both go into their houses in our bedroom whenever I go to bed. Dogs know who takes care of them.]

31 YODA THE YORKSHIRE 'TERROR'

My son decided to teach the bird dog
commands to see if the dogs would obey.

Three wonderful dogs are in my life. Sandy and Taffy
are miniature Dachshunds with brownish red coats.
Their hair is short and their brown eyes expressive.
And Yoda is a loveable Yorkie that came to live with
us. A friend said, "Can you watch him for two
weeks?" and two years later he is still with us. Little
Taffy is a rescued dog. She was found in the desert
and needed a home. She is unable to bark, but it's
interesting how Sandy lets her know what to do.
Sandy is a male dog and larger than Taffy, and she
follows him around all the time. Sometimes if I say,

"Sandy, where is Taffy?"

he'll look around to find her.

Well, one time he could not find her. I could see him walking around the yard circling the pool looking for her. She was unable to bark to let us know where she was so we kept looking. Here in Arizona, it gets very hot in the summer, reaching ranges of 110 and up. Pets can get heat stroke if left out in the heat for very long, so it was important to find her. She could not bark to let us know where she was. It was funny, when we walked around to the side yard, we found her stretched out on a lounge chair relaxing under the umbrella. She looked like she was at a resort.

Another thing that showed me how dogs can understand English is when I took my dogs to get their picture taken with Santa at Christmas. Sandy and Taffy went and also our other dog Yoda.

Yoda is a Yorkshire Terrier, or as my daughter says, "A Yorkshire terror." He is about six pounds of energy but if you say to him,

"YODA! What did you do?"

he will stop and flatten out on the floor and put his paws over his eyes. Then he will peek up at you.

So one day I took them to a local pet store that was promoting getting a Santa photo with pets. Sandy seemed in a bit of a grumpy mood that day. I guess his pride was bothered because I had dressed all three of them in Santa outfits for the occasion. Several times the photographer tried to snap their photo but no one was being good. So I stood in front of them and looked them in the eyes and said,

"When we get this picture taken you will all get treats. Now give me a big smile."

The next photo taken they were all smiling and it looked funny because their teeth were showing in smiles. That was the best pet photo I've ever seen.

Yoda has always been a handful. He gets into everything. One time I was sitting on the sofa just before watching a good movie and Yoda was with me. His favorite spot is next to me no matter what I'm doing. The phone rang and so I set my popcorn bowl on the coffee table and went to answer it. I heard a noise when I was on the phone and so I said loudly,

"YODA! Don't go near the popcorn bowl!"

When I walked back into the room the bowl looked untouched and Yoda was still on the couch looking innocent—except there was a piece of popcorn stuck to his nose when he looked up at me.

Sometimes things happen that are just too funny for words. This was one of those times. We have this beautiful parrot that is quite talkative. His name is Ashley and he sits watching everything in the large family room. The dogs usually ignore the bird unless he squawks. That is until the bird started learning the dogs' names. He would call them and they would come running. My son decided to teach the bird dog commands to see if the dogs would obey. I did not see any response to this until one day as I was folding laundry I heard,

"Yoda, sit," and then "Roll over."

I peeked around the corner and there was Yoda in

front of the bird cage, doing the commands. It was so funny I grabbed the video camera to try to record it, but it was out of charge. Each time the bird would say 'Sit' or 'Roll over', Yoda would do it.

He caught on that it was the bird giving the commands after that, though. I never got another chance to record it. Darn! That would have been a moneymaker, for sure.

[Cherise's note: LOL! I so wish she had gotten that on video! Isn't that hilarious? I wonder if someone else will try it and get it on video and let us know where we can watch it. I would love to see that!]

One of the best examples of a dog understanding English is when I was in the kitchen trying to open a jar. I kept trying and trying with no luck. So I looked down at Sandy and out of exasperation I said,

"I need something to open this."

I didn't pay any attention when he wandered off. But then a few minutes later he came walking up to me and with something in his mouth. He laid it down and it was a wrench. I looked him in the eyes and I could tell he knew what he did. He is one smart little dog.

Dogs are a lot smarter than we give them credit for. They can learn words in English and understand them. Who knows, maybe they can even learn to speak them since they do have vocal cords. They do understand and learn from you, so keep that in mind.

32 ORION THE LABRADOR MIX

*If your paws so much as touch the
linoleum again, you'll be in a world of
trouble!*

I've worked at a veterinary clinic for over 10 years and I admit that every single one of my coworkers and I will talk to the patients as if they understand what we're saying to them. We sometimes use high-pitched voices and talk in baby talk too. We will even hold conversations with them, responding in the voices we think they would have if the dogs and cats could really talk.

This silly work habit often finds its way home with me to my two dogs, Ursa and Orion. Ursa is a 10 year old spayed female Bulldog that I rescued from a shelter when she was 9 months old, and Orion is a 6 year old neutered male Labrador mix that I rescued from my clinic when his original owners abandoned him when he was only 12 weeks old.

On the one hand, Ursa has always been relatively relaxed and not much of a trouble maker. A typical day for her consists of copious amounts of sunbathing and random naps where she drowns out the television with her snoring. She'll raid the trashcan or go counter surfing on the rare occasion but stays out of trouble for the most part. She is also a bit on the pudgy side, but we don't talk about that because she's very sensitive about her weight. She tends to focus her energy on figuring out the best way to get belly rubs in any situation.

Orion, on the other hand, has always been a handful. As a puppy, he was brought to our clinic to be treated for an illness very similar to Parvovirus. After several weeks in our clinic and no word from his original family, I took the little guy home. He was originally going to be named Gatsby after one of my favorite book characters, but after only one night at home, it was perfectly clear that he didn't possess any of the charismatic charm and sophistication of Jay Gatsby. Instead, after successfully tracking down and consuming numerous creepy crawlies, he proved to be a great hunter, and thus he was named Orion the Hunter after the constellation.

I've always believed that most dogs are far smarter than we give them credit for. In my line of work, I have come across numerous animals that have been highly trained. From your basic 'sit, stay, come' commands to the more advanced skills like 'play dead' and 'speak', I've seen it all.

Most dogs are trained to respond to certain words or phrases and are rewarded when they complete the requested action. I've met German Shepherd dogs that only respond to verbal commands spoken in German and other dogs that respond to sign language or hand gestures without a word being spoken. But all of these actions have been ingrained in the dog through repetitive training and rewarding, which is how most dogs are trained. However, I believe there are times when our pets truly understand what we are trying to tell them without the use of training.

As a mother to young children, I'm not a stranger to the fact that kids are messy and dogs are more than eager to clean up after them. My dogs are not the typical 'beggars' though. They don't whine or cry when you have food. The worst that usually happens is that if she's allowed close enough to you, Ursa may drool on your leg. Orion is usually lying in wait for anything to fall on the floor because as anyone with dogs knows, food on the floor is fair game. My dogs have always been allowed in every room of the house, including the kitchen. Their kennel is tucked away in a corner of the kitchen, so they have never been 'trained' to stay out of the kitchen.

Orion is typically my shadow and must be wherever I am. If I move from one room to the next, he'll be sure to follow a minute later. I can't even go to the bathroom without having him wait for me outside the door, and he's not fazed by getting bumped into nearly every time the door opens. It's like I have another toddler, and this one is just furry.

So when I make dinner, Orion is usually somewhere in the kitchen, usually his kennel. On one particularly stressful day, Orion was underfoot as usual while I was making dinner. After multiple attempts to get him to stay out of my way, I calmly informed him,

"If your paws so much as touch the linoleum again, you'll be in a world of trouble!"

So maybe my voice raised a few octaves and there may have been some foot stomping associated with my request, but I never actually spoke a command that he would respond to normally. A moment later, he lay down in the doorway between the carpeted living room and the kitchen. At the time, I was just relieved that he was no longer trying to trip me up like a cat. A few days later, I was once again making dinner and noticed that my shadow wasn't in the kitchen this time.

Orion was lying very quietly in the doorway, his toes right at the edge of the carpet, yet not touching the linoleum.

It must have just been a coincidence, right? No. A week of him sitting in the doorway during dinnertime with his toes hovering above the linoleum but never touching it was surely not a coincidence. To this day, during dinner time, Orion will sit in the doorway. His toes will not touch the linoleum until he is called into the room.

I believe that dogs understand more than we realize. Of course my dog has to be the one trying to be cute and follow my literal directions of not letting his paws touch the linoleum, but I can't even be annoyed at how he likes to try and push the boundaries. We moved recently, and although he is a little more brazen about being in the kitchen when other people are cooking, he will still sit in the doorway with his paws on the threshold whenever I'm the one cooking, as if to say,

"Look, Mom! I remember what you said that one day."

33 TJ THE BRITTANY SPANIEL

No TJ, not here.

My philosophy has always been to speak to animals as if they can understand me. Even if they don't understand the words, animals are highly in tune with their human family members and can usually understand their basic thoughts, concepts, feelings and ideas. Over the years, I have found that in treating them as equal, they often regard my thoughts and feelings on a deeper level and they try hard to understand me.

My Brittany Spaniel was such a dog. I adopted him when he was middle aged for a dog. Overall, he was a happy dog who wanted nothing more than to please me and let me know he loved me. We would take walks together every day, usually at dusk. The reason I rarely walked him during the peak of the day was because he was a bird dog. That meant he wanted to chase anything that moved. It was just his instinct. If he saw a squirrel, bird, cat, rabbit, insect, mouse or any other creature that was moving in his path he wanted to chase them and often hauled me right alongside him. He would simply leap for joy and begin the chase.

I can honestly say until I learned to walk him at dusk I often felt as if I had a case of whiplash just walking him. Dusk is when all the little critters tuck in for the night, so they weren't out there tempting poor TJ to chase them.

[Cherise's note: One of our dogs, Oreo the Springer Spaniel mix, is a hunting dog who cannot resist chasing the squirrels and birds. I hadn't heard of walking them at dusk to avoid this, but during summer I tried it. Sure enough, it works! However, now it's late fall and just too cold by dusk here in Washington State where we live now. Still, this is good to know!]

He was an unusual dog in that he was quite in tune with my human emotions and of those he felt close to me. However, of all the most unique qualities of TJ, I would say the most profound was the sense of utter joy he felt for almost anything and everything. He was certainly not a high maintenance dog, and did not go about acting like a regal king who needed constant dotting after. He was more of a simple fun loving type of dog.

But TJ had a most annoying habit of pooping in the middle of the road while I was walking him down to the little park area just down the street from where I lived. I am certain you can imagine the difficulty I had trying to get him to stop this bad habit. In fact, it was often quite problematic to clean dog poop up out of the middle of the road with cars going by every time I walked him a quarter of a block or so. I tried scolding him, tugging him, coercing him, and praising him for his good efforts, all to get him to stay on the grass for potty and not go in the road, but it still so often failed. Until the day when finally a light switch came on in the mind of TJ.

It started the same as usual. When I was walking him this one particular day and he started to squat the way he always did in the wrong place, I'd had enough and I started lecturing him like he was a teenaged son rather than a dog. I'll bet I looked really funny to anyone who happened to see me, but I really was up to here with having to scoop poop out of the road with cars coming! My lecture sounded something like this:

"No TJ, not here. You are not to go potty in the road. I don't want to clean up your potty in the road with cars going by. It's dangerous. We have to go to the park first, down there on the grass is where you should go potty."

As soon as I said "grass," TJ immediately got up out of his squatting position in the road and leaped right into gear!

He tried to tug me, but he was so desperate to get to the grass that he pulled the leash right out of my hand, then proceeded to run all the way to the grassy knoll of the park. When I finally caught up with him, he sat there waiting patiently for me to arrive, and as soon as he knew I was nearby he found just the right dog spot and went potty.

After months and months of a battle, he went right over to the right area without scolding or coercion. At first I was so shocked I couldn't believe he truly understood me.

But when he repeated the pattern after my statements a few more times I knew he understood completely what I was telling him. There are so many words a dog is trained to learn and understand in commands, but I had rarely seen a dog that was capable of understanding a complete sentence without specific training to do so.

Certainly, over the remaining years of his life, we still had our days when we struggled to get him to go potty in the park and not down in the middle of the road.

This was always a challenge to find a stick to get it out of the road, especially one that wasn't surrounded by poison ivy, or bees. But he definitely got much better after that day, and it seemed from then on that he always knew just what I meant when I piped in with the words,

"No TJ, not here. We have to go to the park first, down there on the grass."

34 MY COLLIE AXLE

IN!

Axle only "understands" what *one* human says. My dog Axle is a Collie and he is about eight months old. Now when you hear me say he is silly and rotten both, I'm not exaggerating. In truth I believe we should have named him goat because no matter what food, bug, item, toy, etc. he sees, he will eat it or at least try to eat it. Makes me want to laugh part of the time and the other makes me a little angry since of course it's something that he isn't supposed to have.

Axle finally started to show he was learning his commands when he was between 3 and 4 months old. I can understand it might have been confusing for him considering he technically has more than one master here where we live. We all kind of share him. There's my daughter, my wife, my wife's father, and myself. My wife's father and I do the same exact actions when it comes to Axle, but for some unknown reason he listens to me more than he does the others. I mean maybe it's because I give him more attention, play with him more, am always teaching him, feeding him, my voice perhaps, or something. Even now, he'll stay right beside me as I eat and obediently he won't try to take my food, but if something drops he's ready to grab it and lap it up. Now with everyone else, he'll listen part of the time. The rest of the time, they'll yell for me to get him under control.

[Cherise's note: "Feeding him" is the key phrase here! Like I said in another story, dogs know who takes care of them, and that person will be the one they're most loyal to. Either that, or if there is a very dominant person in the house, the dogs will sometimes follow that alpha person around and obey their commands first, because of the pack instinct.]

They can take him outside to use the bathroom and he'll run all over the place no matter how many times they say, "Axle, no." I can take him outside and he'll go no more than maybe 30 feet away from me, do what he needs to do, come right back to me, and stand at the door ready for me to let him in.

He also will literally follow me around like a little puppy. Brings a smile to my face majority of the time, but there are a few times it bothers me because I'm trying to do something that's very important and he gets in the way.

Especially if I have to go to the bathroom. If I'd let him, he'd go in with me. Only problem is, if I do he's all over me and his claws do hurt. Of course he doesn't mean to hurt anyone. He can't help it that his claws are pointy.

When he knows I'm getting ready to go out the door to leave for my eight hours at work, he acts just like a child would. He doesn't jump on me, but he'll stand on his hind legs and very accurately wrap his front arms around my leg and give me one of the saddest looks I've ever seen a dog give. The first time he ever did that it truly surprised me because:

1) As soon as I felt him clench, I thought I was going to get scratched for sure.

2) He didn't scratch me.

3) I have never had a dog do that so accurately as if to give me a hug with a look of, "I don't want you to go."

4) It was just like my own child saying goodbye.

There was a command that I had given and in truth hadn't expected him to get right off as he was only about 3 months old. He has his own cage that's more for sleeping at night, but also used if he does something bad.

[Cherise's note: We never use our dogs' crates for discipline. We call their crate their house, and it is their sanctuary where they can go to feel safe. We only lock them in there for their own good, such as when we're vacuuming, or when we have company in the winter, because they are guard dogs and it's too cold for them to be outside.]

Well, one night Axle wasn't listening to anyone and I was at work. I apparently came home at the right moment because he was in trouble for getting into the trash. From what they told me, they all had warned him and said, "No" to no avail. When I came home, they were trying to get him in his cage without having to push him or anything. They were also trying to teach him the word 'in' at the same time.

They heard me come home, and they all came to me to explain what had happened. Well, while they were talking to me, Axle started to get into the trash again, but I caught him. I yelled, "No!" He stopped. Then they told me again that they were trying to get him into the cage and to teach him a new command, 'In', at the same time. I said, "I'll try, but it probably won't work at first because we haven't tried it before."

I called Axle over to me in front of the cage, and with a stern voice I pointed into the cage and said, "IN!"

To my utmost surprise, he ducked downward, kept his nose straight forward, and walked on in! I had to reassemble my mind because it had caught me off guard, him listening so well with a new thing. I crouched down, patted him on his head, and said, "See you in the morning, Buddy." I was so proud he had listened to me on the first try, it was hard to keep him in the cage. But that was what everyone else had decided, and I wasn't going to go against them.

Axle has his bad moments, but good just the same. One of the ways he's rotten and very playful is when we play fetch. I'll throw whatever toy he brings me, and as we had taught him, he goes, retrieves it, and brings it back to me.

After a few times, he'll retrieve it and instead of bringing it to me he'll run right to me and change his course at the last second to dodge me, then he comes back. I have come to find out that he himself is trying to make it more interesting. He's actually wanting me to try and grab the toy as he's passing by. Took quite a few games to see what he was wanting. He will also, instead of bringing it to me or dodging, lunge at me with the toy wanting me to catch him.

He's also a fan of tug-of-war. He will hold onto it until he's almost in the air, then he'll release and either wait for me to throw it, or jump up and grab it again.

For the most part he is a very energetic and happy dog, almost always wagging his tail and just playing with us, or just prancing around the house. Very seldom is he being bad, or being sad.

I have figured out that when he's doing something bad, it's not that he doesn't know better. It's because he's wanting attention.

35 MY POMERANIAN TOBY

Go to Danny and sit on his lap.

Toby is a wonder dog and he has always been treated like a child. This year he will turn 8 and he is getting up there in years. As a small house dog, a Pomeranian, I needed him most when I was having issues with panic and anxiety. We purchased him when he was 8 months old from my aunt who was dying of cancer. Funny thing is, the family pitched in and purchased him for her to provide comfort in her lonely hours. In return, I ended up with him, and comfort he did.

When my husband would work night shift, I noticed how special Toby was. He became my "main man." I actually started seeing how jealous he was right away. He would not allow my husband near me and when he would come in too close of a range, he would bark and growl. When my husband would have a night off from his night shift job, Toby didn't like this. One night, my husband crawled in bed and jumped right out again, quite perturbed. It seemed that Toby had left a little brown package on his pillow for him. It seems this was deliberate.

This all happened when Toby was under a year old. I often would threaten him that I was going to put him in the local newspaper. It seemed this dog always had a "special package" just waiting to drop it in anger. When we would shut the bedroom door to be alone, there would always be a package lying just outside the bedroom doorway. This was his calling card. When he turned 1 year old, we started realizing how smart he truly was, too smart for his own good. I truly think Toby understands what we are saying, both to him and to each other.

As a puppy, he loved toys. Every time I would go out shopping I would bring this little cute puppy a new toy. There were two toys that he loved the most, a giraffe and a frog. The giraffe was nick-named Raf-raf and the frog was called Little Froggy. Toby loved to play with these and shake them to pieces. They were not dog toys, as he chewed them all up, but rather toys from the local dollar store. He loved to play fetch and would often bring them to one or both of us to play with him. He continues this same habit after 8 years.

During play, I noticed that I could call the name of a toy and he would go get that specific toy. I thought it was weird. He had many toys, including the whole singing Taco Bell dog collection. He loved to press their buttons and hear them sing.

I wanted to see how much this dog knew. It turns out he knows the name of every toy! When I say,

"Raf-raf, where are you?"

Toby will turn his head from side to side like he understands, and then he'll go get his toy giraffe. The first time he did this, I thought, "Now wait a minute! This dog's a genius!" He has since lost interest in all of his toys, but he will still go get that same tattered yellow giraffe to this day.

I noticed toys are not his only acknowledgment of human language. There're other things. Whenever he wants to climb into bed with us, he'll sit patiently by the side of the bed waiting. He'll maybe scratch a couple times, but I know he's already been outside. If it's OK for him to get into bed, then I look at him and say,

"Permission to enter,"

and Toby jumps up on the bed. To this day, he still waits patiently beside the bed and waits for me to say "Permission to enter."

He absolutely adores riding in the car and would do anything for a trip. The girls at McDonalds all know him and so does our local bank. After 8 years, he is still one amazingly cute pup and he still loves to wear his shirts. There are some times when I simply cannot take this dog with me in the car. I mean Wal-Mart and other stores won't allow pets. But as soon as the door opens, he would always run to the car and jump in before I could say otherwise.

I had to fix this quickly.

Rather than saying 'bye-byes', which seems to get him all in a tizzy, I thought the word 'no' should be used. I started telling Toby either yes or no when it came to me leaving. I would put my finger up and shake it while saying the word no. Now, when it is time for me to leave, I either say,

"Come on, let's go bye-byes," or "No," with the finger shaking.

He cocks his head from side to side and will go lie back down if the answer is no.

[Cherise's note: I do something similar with our dogs, only it's either "Yeah! We're going for a walk!" or "No, you stay here." When I tell the dogs, "No, you stay here," they come up to be petted goodbye and then go lie down. They get so excited if the answer is "Yeah! We're going for a walk!" that I have a hard time putting my shoes on, they are so busy licking my face, LOL!]

There is no one in this world that Toby loves better than me. When I return home in my van, he always comes flying out the door and into the van, tail wagging to see me. If I say,

"Give Momma a kiss,"

he sticks out his little tongue and kisses my cheek with his licks. I swear I have never seen a dog so smart in my life. He knows the kids' names and he will go to each one if I tell him to. Sometimes, I will improvise and say something like,

"Go to Danny and sit on his lap," or "Go to

Sandy and lick her hand,"

and Toby does just that.

Perhaps one of the funniest things is that Toby knows my husband and me by the terms Mommy and Daddy.

He also knows quite well the phrase, 'Your spot'. His spot is right beside me on my pillow, and he will turn his paws toward me like we are snuggling. He likes to wander around the bed, lick my husband's bald head and just explore other sleeping positions and places. All I have to do to get my snuggle partner back is say,

"Toby, come get in your spot."

I know Toby is getting up in years, and I have been told he has an enlarged heart. I have never had such a bond or an experience of this nature with such a wonderful animal. I don't know what I will do when he passes on. I can't imagine the day when I come home and he is not there. Statistically he has 8-10 year life span, but I pray for much more. There has never been a dog as wonderful as Toby, and there never will be.

36 GUS THE PIT BULL

I told Pops I was scared and he told me it was worth a shot, anyway.

This story takes us back eight years to a time when I had my Pit Bull dog named Gus. Gus was mostly a laid-back kind of dog. Although he would go through times of being hyper, especially as I stepped off the bus coming home from school. He was excited to see me, and we would always play for a bit before I would go in to get my homework done for the day. Gus always stayed outside, for Momma wouldn't allow him in the house. He was just way too big and loved to get dirty from rolling around in the dirt all day.

Gus was a family dog though. Any time Pops and I would go fishing or out on the boat, Gus was always allowed to go with us. Even when we went on long vacation trips to see my grandparents, he got to come too.

Every time we were getting ready to go out of state, I was in control of giving Gus a bath to ensure he was completely clean before hopping in the truck. When he was all bathed he looked absolutely gorgeous. He was a brindle Pit, so his colors were absolutely amazing and the gold in his coat really stood out. His collar was red and looked amazing on him. Although Gus looked big and mean, he was the best dog that anyone could ask for and was super protective of me. We were best friends, and that's the way it's supposed to be.

One day I remember coming home and my parents weren't there yet. They had to work late, but I was old enough to take care of myself for a while when they did have to work late occasionally. I remember getting off the bus from school and Gus didn't greet me at the gate like he normally did. I didn't really think about it because like I said, he was the type to be a laid-back pup. I went on into the house and did my homework like I always did as soon as I got home. It was just so much easier to get it over with so I didn't have to think about it for the rest of the evening.

After my homework was finished, I noticed that Momma had left me a note on the counter to get the laundry started and lay out the meat for supper. So I did as she said in the note. Also, she stated that I needed to get washed up and ready to go to bed for the evening. Since I was focused on the chores that Momma had left me, I didn't have the time to go see what Gus was up to. By the time Momma and Pops got home, they were completely worn out and ready to get supper over with. After we all ate they were ready to relax for the evening and get to bed soon.

The next morning I woke up early so I could see Gus before I took off for school again and make sure he was fed for the day. When I got ready and went outside he was nowhere to be found. I panicked and looked all over the yard for him. I thought that maybe he just went to sleep somewhere and was being lazy. It wasn't like Gus to run away, but then again you never know. I couldn't find him anywhere. I ran in the house to get Momma and Pops so they could help me find Gus. They panicked too, for Gus was a really good dog and we wanted to find him so he could be safe. They were unable to find him that morning either. Momma made me hurry up and get my things together so I wouldn't miss the bus and promised she would do what she could to find him.

That afternoon, Pops came and got me out of class early. It was a Friday anyway. We didn't do much in class on Fridays. He had a bunch of signs made up so we could post them around our small town. It took us several hours to go to each business and hang them in the windows as well as on the poles all over the town. Once we finished we returned home to get ready for supper again and wait by the phone.

The next morning we received a call that a man was seen in town with a dog that looked just like ours. Pops and I jumped in the truck to go see if the dog was our Gus. We went into town and saw a dog that looked just like Gus. The man refused to give him to us. He said,

"The only way I'll let you have him is if the dog responds to you calling him by his name."

Gus wasn't used to responding to commands, for he never had to. He was an outside pet and didn't get commanded that often. I was scared that when I yelled his name he would just sit there. I told Pops I was scared and he told me it was worth a shot, anyway.

I yelled out, "Gus, come here, Boy!"

and sure enough, Gus jumped up on all fours and ran to me. He was happy as ever. The man then believed it was our dog and released him to us. Pops thanked him for his time and we were on our way home. That night I stayed with Gus for as long as I could. Then Momma made me come in of course. I have never been so happy to know that Gus really did understand his name and came to me by command. I'll never forget how I found my dog again and what it meant to me to have him back home and safe.

[Cherise's note: None of our dogs ever ran away or got nabbed, thank God. I did have a cat that once went missing. She was gone for two weeks, and I had given up on ever seeing her again. One of my friends worried me even more by reminding me, "After this long, she might not even remember you." But she did remember. She did come home and meow loudly outside my door. For the first ten minutes, she didn't know whether to be in my lap getting petted or at her dish eating.]

37 PEACHES THE COCKERPOO MUD PUPPY

Peaches or Mud Puppy?

When we were kids, my younger sister Kendra and I always conned my parents into buying us a pet or two. My dad always claimed he couldn't stand animals (but would be found secretly petting them from time to time), while my mom was mostly indifferent. Our parents' lack of interest in pets was always amusing to me, as my sister and I were extreme animal fanatics.

One of our favorite pets was Peaches, a whip smart Cockerpoo (that is, half Cocker Spaniel and half Toy Poodle), that always seemed to uncannily understand you. She also had amazing survival skills, and looked both ways before crossing the road. No kidding. She would look left, right, and then left again, and jog across the road if it was clear. She wouldn't cross until the road was free from cars. This wasn't something we taught her. She learned it on her own.

She also learned tricks faster than any other dog I've ever owned. With a box of dog bones, my sister and I taught her to sit in about 10 minutes. I'd say, "Sit." Kendra would push her butt down, and I'd hand her a bone. After about 10 bones, she sat without getting her butt pushed down. She learned 'shake' in the same way.

[Cherise's note: From the TV shows my husband watches, I now know that 'shake' is supposed to command the dog to shake water off its fur, and that the dog is supposed to wait until you give the command so it doesn't get you soaked when it shakes.]

The most amazing "English comprehension" moment we had with Peaches was the "Mud Puppy" incident. When we were about 14 and 12, my parents owned some land on the river. They had a trailer, an outhouse, and a few acres of cleared land. We used to spend nearly every summer there, with my various aunts and uncles coming to visit for days on end. Cousins, nephews, and friends also visited for days.

Peaches always came too, and she loved to go swimming with us. That always confused me, as she always seemed to hate baths worse than anything else. But, she'd follow my sister and me into the river, follow us along the banks as we floated down the river, and play fetch with us in the water. She always got muddy, so we'd have to clean her off. It was worth it.

One day, my niece Holly was staying down at the river with us. Holly was around my age, as her dad was much older than me, and we were best friends growing up. We did everything together, along with her brother Dusty, and summers were always the best time of the year for us. We never seemed to stop having fun together.

It was an incredibly hot day, the kind of day that makes swimming inevitable. We spent a few hours splashing in the river, and loyal, dependable Peaches was right there with us. Mom and Dad visited with Ray and Sue, Holly's parents. They grilled burgers and hot dogs as we played, and the smell kept us near the house. We didn't want to miss Ray's legendary grilled burgers!

Once we were finished, we ran up the shore, followed closely by Peaches. She was muddy from head to toe, but we didn't clean her immediately. The mud was wet, and it helped keep her cool. She always had a lot of hair, and it seemed like it was the nice thing to do for her.

The four of us, Kendra, Holly, Peaches, and I, walked to the picnic table near the trailer and sat down. We were dripping wet and still laughing from playing earlier. A bowl of chips sat on the table, and we snacked regularly. Peaches watched us eagerly, waiting for a chip to fall. She didn't have to wait long. We gladly gave her chips.

Holly looked down at Peaches with a chip in her hand, and laughed. "Peaches, you look just like a mud puppy!" she said. Peaches wagged her stub of a tail so hard, her entire body shook. Holly grabbed two chips, and held one in each hand. "Watch this," she said. "Peaches?" she said, lifting the chip in her right hand in the air, "or Mud Puppy?" she said, lifting the chip in her left hand. Peaches immediately ate the 'mud puppy' chip. We all laughed, and Holly did it again.

Once again, Peaches ate the chip in her left hand.

"She likes 'Mud Puppy'!" Holly said.

"She keeps picking the left chip," I said, always the cynic. "It's closest to her."

"OK, OK," said Holly. "Peaches," she said, lifting the chip in her left hand, "or Mud Puppy?" she said lifting the chip in her right.

To our surprise, Peaches still immediately ate the 'mud puppy' chip, this time in Holly's right hand.

"Do it again!" I said, surprised it had worked.

Holly repeated the actions again, once again assigning 'mud puppy' to her right hand. Peaches ate the right hand chip.

We repeated the action over and over again, changing the location of the 'mud puppy' chip repeatedly. Holly would do mud puppy on the left twice, then on the right three times. Sometimes, she'd alternate the sides one chip at a time. We did it so many times that we emptied the bowl, feeding Peaches chips. And every time Holly held up the chips, Peaches chose 'Mud Puppy.'

We tried to tell our parents the story, but they didn't believe us.

"You feed that whole bowl of chips to the dog?" said my dad. "You aren't getting any more chips today," he said with a deadpan face as he opened up a fresh back of chips and refilled the bowl.

The strangest part about all of this was that Peaches pulled a repeat of the trick years later. Holly once again held the chips, and Peaches chose 'Mud Puppy' every time. It really makes you wonder about dogs.

[Cherise's note: I wonder if it would have been different had Holly said, "Mud Puppy, or Peaches?"]

38 OUR GOLDEN RETRIEVER ROCKET

Company!

Being an adult has its perks, but I don't think I've grown up much since I was a kid. Video games, cartoons, soda; these are all things my roommates and I do on a daily basis. I guess you can say that we all haven't grown up much. Unfortunately being a kid at heart doesn't very much get our bills paid, and nowadays minimum wage jobs aren't really enough to suffice for a good income. Even though we're still young, we wanted to start living our own lives, so we packed up and got our own apartment. Now to pay the bills we had to settle for a cramped living space. In other words, there's six of us living in a small three bedroom apartment. We have Tyler, Stephen, Josh, Kyle, and myself, Anthony.

Who is the sixth fellow you might ask? Well, he's more of a person to us than a pet, but number six on our team is our Golden Retriever, Rocket. Rocket is a great dog and an even greater friend, especially on our bad days. I've had Rocket since I was in high school, but the guys all adopted him like he was their own within the first week of moving in.

Now don't get me wrong. Rocket has his downsides too. Tearing through Kyle's homework, leaving shed hair everywhere, using our PlayStation controllers as chew toys; the list goes on. What's worse is that he isn't even a puppy anymore. This is just how Rocket is.

But he's mostly great. At the age of four years old (human years) he hails to be one playful, understanding, messy, and amazing dog. We couldn't ask for a better pet, and Rocket has always been good at listening (minus the puppy years), but on one occasion Rocket comprehended something said that floored all of us.

Being the lovely bachelors that we are, it's probably already assumed that we keep a severely messy house. Dishes to the roof, clothes on the floor, you name it; we have it. The only time we adamantly clean is if we're planning on having company over. Whoever winds up bringing over a friend or a family member will get all of our attention and say something along the lines of,

"Alright, company!"

and we'll all understand that it's time to get to work.

It was funny too, watching Rocket react to this at first. He'd know that something was going on, run around in circles as if he wanted to help, and then just sit down with us whenever we finished picking up.

We have company over quite a bit as well, being

on our own and such, especially me. I'm the social butterfly of the house. I mean it was even my idea to have six of us live together. Anyway, as I scheduled more visits, Rocket stuck to his same routine: running around in circles until we were done and then contentedly sitting down.

This lasted for about four months, until one day Rocket stopped running around. The word 'company' ran through the air and even after seeing all of us fumble about, Rocket chose to lie down and watch us. We all made confused faces at each other seeing the lazy dog watch without a care in the world. We thought something was wrong at first, but he was perfectly fine. We wound up coming to the conclusion that he'd gotten used to us cleaning. With our beloved pup's newfound routine underway, it actually made cleaning up a bit easier to do. Have you ever tried to do something while your dog was in the way? It's a bit challenging if you ask me. After another month or two passed, we would still be doing our bi-weekly to monthly pick up for company, adjusting to the new Rocket routine.

One day though we had an unexpected visitor: our landlord.

We dreaded seeing our landlord. It was as if he always had something to pick and say about us. He gave me a phone call stating that he was on his way over to check up on the meters at the house and a few faucets inside. Everyone heard the phone call. I looked up at everyone and said,

"Company,"

in the most melancholy tone you'd ever hear.

Everyone knew from my voice that I meant the landlord. No matter what we did, there was no pleasing him, and it was for this very reason that we didn't have the motivation to clean for him. Instead we all chose to sit and dreadfully await his arrival.

All of us that is, except for Rocket. After a few minutes passed by, Rocket seemed a bit restless from where he was lying. He whimpered and whined and eventually got up and left the living room. Not long after, we started hearing some rustling.

"I'll check it out," I told everyone, thinking that he was getting into trouble.

I walked into our bedroom to find that Rocket was actually cleaning!

At least he was trying to anyway. Picking up the clothes on the floor with his mouth only to put them on the bed I would definitely count as cleaning. I couldn't believe it. After all the times hearing us say the word 'company', Rocket actually understood that people were coming over. I called the guys in and showed them what our dog was doing. They were all as baffled as I was.

A lot of people think that dogs are just pets, but not us. Our dog is a person, just like we are, and he definitely proved that as he helped pick up the mess that we all made.

39 FOX, A GERMAN SHEPHERD

Hide.

Can any of you remember Lassie, and how intelligent we thought she was? Well I had a German Shepherd (supposedly mixed with wolf) that was right up there with her on the highly intelligent dog level.

I got Fox when he was just an eight week old puppy, and I was just sixteen years old. He came from an animal rescue type place called PAWS. However, this was not a very good place for any cat or dog. The people that ran PAWS back in the 1970s did as well as they could to take care of the many unwanted animals. But things quickly got out of hand and soon the dogs and puppies were kept tied up all year round, and some of the puppies grew ill and passed away.

I am telling you this because to know Fox, you have to know where he came from. I loved dogs my entire life and was in love with the German Shepherd breed, so I was searching for a German Shepherd puppy to raise. During a visit to PAWS I saw Fox at eight weeks old, chained to an old falling down dog house. He looked and acted like a typical lonely puppy, and to me, he appeared to be a full blood German Shepherd. I decided right then and there that this was going to be the puppy I bought and brought home, so I paid the twenty-five dollars for him and brought him home, despite my mother's concern that he hadn't had any sort of vet care and had been around other puppies and dogs that were ill. Thankfully Fox turned out to be extremely healthy when he had his vet visit to get a checkup and to receive his puppy shots.

It was not long before I came to realize that there was something very different about Fox even as a young puppy. From the very first day I brought him home, the puppy would watch every move I made very carefully. Normal dog type games such as fetch and tug a war bored him. So every day I would take him to the local park and work with him on obedience training. Unlike other puppies his age, Fox caught on to every word and what it meant within two days' time. People would often stop what they were doing to watch as I taught Fox how to play games like hide and seek just like a human.

I would tell Fox, "Hide" and point at a tree.

He would then run behind the tree and remain hidden until I found him. No amount of calling Fox while playing this game would bring him out of his hiding spot. He had to be found and tapped on the head.

'You're it' he understood to mean it was my turn to hide, and he would have to find me.

Fox and I quickly learned new things for him to do such as: swing on the swings by himself, play dead when I shot him with my finger, 'Go back', 'Go back and lie down right there', 'Go back and turn around twice, then lie down.'

Fox's favorite word and favorite thing to do was to 'Take' and 'Carry' items of all types. He would carry my suitcase up a flight of stairs, or he would carry his very own large bone from the butcher.

As Fox grew older, he and I traveled to different states, and once I had proven how highly intelligent my dog was, he would be allowed to lie at my feet in restaurants and was welcomed into motels that never allowed pets of any kind into their rooms.

My favorite time was when we had to travel by Greyhound bus from Idaho to get back home to Washington State. I was a bit concerned that no matter how good Fox was, we would not be allowed on the bus. So I came up with an idea of how to get Fox to do one of his best tricks.

I found a box large enough for a six month old German Shepherd to hide in. When I told Fox to 'Hide' he leaped into the box and hid his face as best he could. My mother and I carried the box onto the bus and sat it on a seat right in front of where we were sitting. About three hours into the ride, the bus driver became suspicious when he saw me putting a bowl of water into the box. He stopped the bus and very slowly walked over to my seat and looked into the box.

Seeing the anger on his face at finding a large German Shepherd on his bus, I told Fox,

"Hide."

Fox quickly lowered his head and shoulders so that he was hidden again inside the box.

The bus driver burst out laughing.

Needless to say, Fox was a hit and we were allowed to enjoy our Greyhound bus ride all the way to Washington State, so long as we would entertain the passengers with the things Fox could do.

I have had many dogs since owning my Fox, but to this day there has never been another one that could understand everything I said, and I guess there never will be.

[Cherise's note: Don't you love that the dog played hide and seek? If we ever have a big enough yard again to do that, I'm going to try it with our dogs. A game that Raffle will play is 'Run, run, run!' I pretend I'm trying to catch him and I lunge at him and say, "Run, run, run!" He runs off past me, trying to escape, and then he comes charging at me and I lunge at him again. I made up this game with Raffle when he was a puppy so that he would get exercise and not just sit in the yard all the time. This was back before I took daily walks. I tried to get Oreo, our other dog, to play 'Run, run, run!' but he just sits there and looks at me like I'm being an idiot, LOL!]

40 BELLA MY YORKSHIRE TERRIER

Bella, go play soccer.

Bella is a furry and fuzzy little Yorkshire Terrier who's full of personality, to say the least. She always responds to normal commands, as all dogs do: 'Sit', 'Stay', 'Heel'. Well, most of the time she responds. Sometimes Bella is feeling extra spunky and decides that she'll just do her own thing. She's a free spirit for sure.

It just so happens that one day I discovered that she understood a little more than regular dog commands. She's obviously been listening to everything and everyone around her and she's got us all figured out. Bella has got the upper hand (or paw) on us humans. My dog understands English!

When Bella was just a puppy, she was given a small stuffed lion. The lion was just small enough for her to carry around everywhere, and its mane was sturdy enough to withstand it being dragged around by the head. Bella took the lion everywhere she went, and only occasionally put the lion down to lick or gently bite a visitor. One day the lion went missing. I searched high and low for this thing but I could not find it. I looked under the couch, in the laundry room, behind the television. I looked in all of Bella's normal hang out and hiding spots. No lion. Finally one night as I was putting Bella to bed, my foot brushed up against a soft plush toy that was just under my bed. The lion had reemerged.

I let Bella get her beauty rest that night and didn't disturb her with news of the lion's return. The next morning after Bella had her breakfast, I brought the lion out and placed it in the middle of the floor. Bella looked at it like it was some foreign creature that she had never seen before. This couldn't have been the lion that she cherished so much just days before, but it was! After watching Bella deliberate over whether or not to approach the lion, I finally said,

"Bella, get your baby."

As soon as she heard me say this she ran toward the lion, scooped it up in her mouth, tossed it in the air a few times and then grabbed it again, running around with it for minutes. When she tired of this, she rolled on her back with the lion in her mouth and clutched it with her petite paws. Moments before, Bella had been reluctant to be reunited with her beloved doll, but once I invited her to reclaim her 'baby', she gladly resumed her relationship with her little lion. It was as if they had never parted.

Of course, that's just one incident. On another occasion, though, she did the same thing, this time with another toy. Bella had also been given a neon green soccer ball as a puppy. She would play with the ball on and off. Sometimes it would frustrate her because it was more than half her size, almost taller than her. Bella, undeterred, would grab the ball with her teeth and drag it as far as she could before giving in to fatigue. One day, when she had become more comfortable with handling the ball, I jokingly said,

"Bella, go play soccer."

To my surprise, she sprang into action and got the soccer ball and began throwing it into the air, kicking it and even barking at it like it was an unruly teammate in a real soccer game. It was absolutely hilarious. Bella was transformed into some sort of gifted soccer dog. Up to this point I had never commanded Bella to play soccer, so there was no way she was simply following a command. Bella totally understood not only what I was saying to her, but also what the game of soccer involved. I think she might be an undercover super-dog.

As if that weren't enough to make me believe that my pup understands English perfectly, Bella showed me a few more times that she knows just what is being said, especially when it's about her. One day I was on the phone with my sister and Bella decided that she wasn't getting enough attention from me. She began pawing me and when that didn't get results, she started barking. When I shushed her she calmed down for a while. Then she began her tantrum once more. Again I told her to quiet down and she obeyed.

A few minutes later the conversation between my sister and I turned to Bella.

The only thing is, I never used her name.

I was talking about how she had chased another dog, believing that she was bigger than she really is. I spoke about her nightly ritual of running into every room in the house before settling into her bed. I mentioned how I would have to be more diligent about her obedience training. I mentioned that she had been making so much noise in the background before and now she had settled down and was resting like nothing ever happened. I had a whole five minute conversation about Bella, but I never ever said her name.

My sister, on the other end of the line, may have said Bella's name, but I never did. Despite this, Bella was aware that I was talking about her in her face. The entire time that I gossiped about her, Bella's ears were perked up and she had trotted over to where I was sitting and was staring in my face as if to say,

"I know you're talking about me."

It was pretty funny. I described the scene to my sister who agreed that Bella must be aware that I was chatting about her. Needless to say, we both had a good laugh.

Yes, my Bella is a smarty pants. She can go far beyond simple dog commands and interpret the English language quite well, even when no one is talking directly to her. She's truly amazing!

[Cherise's note: I'm sure Bella could hear the sister saying her name, through the phone line and across the room. Still, it's cute to imagine Bella looking indignant over being gossiped about!]

41 KITTA THE GERMAN SHEPHERD

*Sorry, Girl. I can't get up. I need my
knee brace.*

My dog Kitta understands a lot more than I expected
her to. She is able to understand things that I did not
think she would be able to recognize or remember.

On Friday nights my family does movie night. We
cook dinner together and rent a movie. With the
movie comes popcorn. We eat the popcorn and
watch some silly movies. As a member of the family,
Kitta is involved in movie night. One Friday as we
were eating popcorn, Kitta sat there trying to beg for
food. Instead of just giving it to her, my son threw it
up in the air to see if she could catch it. She did. She
came back for more popcorn and seemed to really
like it as a treat. After that, every movie night she
would join us in front of the TV and wait for the
popcorn to be made.

One day I went food shopping and purchased a

box of popcorn among other things that we needed to eat for the week. I was unpacking the bag and put the box of popcorn on the kitchen table with other items that were going to be stored in the cabinet. So that I could put it away without having to walk back to the table, I asked my son,

"Get me the box of popcorn."

To my great surprise, Kitta—who of course was in the room since the food was around—went up to the table and grabbed the box of popcorn! She brought it over to me and whined a little bit. I had no idea that she was going to be able to know the word 'popcorn' and grab the correct box. I was surprised that she could understand English let alone read English.

[Cherise's note: We know that Kitta smelled which box had the popcorn in it, rather than reading the box. But it sure is cute that her owner thought she could read! ☺]

Another time, my aunt came over for a visit. It is easy to say that she is not a dog person. She does not see a dog as a member of the family but rather a pet. She thinks that all pets should stay outside and are just animals.

That is not true for my family. Kitta sleeps in bed with me most of the time. Other nights I find her getting comfortable on the couch. Kitta is allowed to sit on the couch as well. She likes to sit close to the family.

My aunt sat on the couch and made herself comfortable. She had not paid any attention to Kitta since she came into our home. She did not even pet the dog.

Kitta does not like being ignored. Everyone has to love and acknowledge her or she will not rest until they pet her. When she went to sit on the couch right next to my aunt I was not surprised at all.

My aunt turned to the dog and yelled, "Get this mongrel away from me."

We have never used words like that when referring to Kitta. Kitta turned to my aunt and snorted at her. She also gave her a nasty look. We all found it funny because between the snort and the look it was like she was telling my aunt, "Buzz off."

My aunt just looked at her, surprised that she fully understood her and her reaction. I thought this was one of the funniest things that I have ever seen. We all had a good laugh at this but we still have no idea where she learned that word, 'mongrel' and knew that it meant something that was not too nice. I wish I'd gotten a video of this.

[Cherise's note: The aunt's tone of voice and body language would have been plenty of information for the dog to know the aunt wasn't being nice, without having to know the word, 'mongrel', but I love that Kitta snorted at the aunt!]

I used to play field hockey in high school. Twenty years later I still like to watch the sport but it has taken a toll on my knee. Every now and then it really acts up to the point that I am not able to walk. When this happens I have a knee brace that I can put on it.

The brace makes the pain bearable, but it still hurts and I can't do my normal activities. Kitta knew something was up when I didn't take her for our evening walk. We walk every day, even when it's raining.

I was sitting on the couch and it hurt to get up. I wanted to get my brace but it was upstairs in the bedroom. No one was around but Kitta. She was sitting at my feet. She began to bark and I had a feeling she knew that it was time for her walk and she wanted to go already. I started to talk to her and mentioned,

"Sorry, Girl. I can't get up. I need my knee brace."

All of a sudden she gets up and goes upstairs. She comes back down a minute to two later with my knee brace in her mouth.

She was able to understand what I needed and went up to get it for me. Even though it hurt, I was so impressed that I put it on and was able to take her for a short walk. I was very surprised by this. I did not know that dogs were able to understand the names of parts of the human body.

[Cherise's note: I don't think Kitta understood 'knee'. I think she recognized 'knee brace' from hearing the humans talk about it. What's amazing to me about this one is that Kitta understood what 'I need' meant.]

42 MUNCHKIN MY PEKINGESE

Munch, where is that stupid remote?

When I was a police officer, I used to see how K-9 officers [dogs are canines, get it?] would respond to their police handlers' verbal commands. A good way to see how smart dogs are and see how well they can understand you is by watching police dogs understand their handlers.

Pekingese dogs used to belong to kings in Japan. As such, they are very high maintenance. They are good dogs but they are also stubborn dogs, and sometimes when they make up their minds it can be a very strong battle of wills. Even so, the old saying that a dog is a man's best friend is very true, and a dog and his handler can sometimes become inseparable.

I rescued Munchkin from the animal shelter when he was a little puppy. When I first got him he was filled with fleas but I cleaned him up nice and good and he was a very happy dog. When I used to come home I would sit on the couch and Munchkin would jump up in my lap and watch television with me. Many nights I would have to search my room for my remote and a lot of times I could not find it. Of course most nights it would turn up sooner or later.

One night when I came home I put all of my groceries away and Munchkin was sitting on the kitchen floor looking up at me. I looked around and said to Munch,

"Are you ready to go out?"

Munch's ears perked up and his tail started wagging. As I went to find his leash he ran and sat down by the door, waiting for me. Once I got his leash on we went downstairs and took his usual walk.

As we walked I was still training him on how to heel because he liked to take the lead, and as a handler I was supposed to take the lead because there can only be one alpha in a pack. In our pack of two, that was supposed to be me. It was almost like a game to Munchkin. I would take the lead but he would run up in front of me and I would have to take the lead again, and back and forth we went.

The same night that we went for the walk we came back upstairs. After we got settled in we sat up on the couch as we usually did. I turned the television on and looked for my remote and as usual I could not find it anywhere. I searched the whole living room. I checked on the counter, behind the television on the floor and even under the couch. I looked over at Munchkin who was looking at me with a weird look on his face like he was asking, "What are you doing?"

In my aggravation and not at all expecting any response, I called out to Munchkin,

"Munch, where is that stupid remote?"

Munchkin jumped off the couch and ran into my bedroom downstairs. I continued searching for that stupid remote and talking to myself. All of a sudden I heard Munchkin barking. I yelled at Munchkin to stop barking. Not all my neighbors liked to hear dogs barking at night, and I was frustrated with not being able to find my remote.

Now just so you know, it never clicked in my head that Pekingese dogs don't bark that much.

Munchkin came running back to the living room and started barking again and took off back down the stairs. At this point I was getting frustrated with his barking so I had to go see what was going on.

When I walked into the bedroom that Munchkin was in he was standing in a corner staring out the window. I walked over to Munchkin and asked him what was wrong and turned on the light. I still did not know what Munchkin was barking at. Munchkin went and stood over by the window and lay on the floor, so I went over there by him and sat down on the floor beside him and started rubbing his belly.

While rubbing his belly I noticed the remote sitting under the nightstand by the window.

Munchkin had found my remote. I was shocked. I couldn't believe it. Not only was he able to understand that I couldn't find my remote, but he also found it for me!

If he'd been a bigger dog that could get his mouth around the remote, then I know he would have brought it to me. As it was, he made me come in and see where I must have dropped it the night before.

I know a lot of people don't believe that dogs understand what people are saying, but if you think about it, dogs certainly do understand. When a handler tells their dog to 'sit', 'heel' or 'roll over', the dog understands what those commands mean. Even if it is taught by habit, they still understand.

Dogs are very loyal animals and they are very smart. Think about when you call your dog's name. Do your dog's ears perk up when you call them? Dogs do understand some things that we say, and Munchkin proved it to me that day we were looking for my missing remote.

[Cherise's note: I don't know if the dog even needed to know the word 'remote' in this situation. His human played with the thing every evening. He must have seen his human carry the thing into the bedroom the night before and drop it there. The human was fond of this thing. I don't think it's much of a stretch at all for the dog to have realized what the human wanted just based on the human's normal nightly playing with this thing. I do think it is really sweet that the dog decided to help the human find his toy rather than play dumb, which is what our dog Oreo would probably do. Our dog Raffle probably would help us find our lost toy.]

43 MY GERMAN SHEPHERD BREEZY

Go home and get help!

I was 13 years old at the time this story happened, and I lived on the island of Oahu in Hawaii. I had lived there my whole life and grew up with my best friend Breezy. Breezy was a full bred German Shepherd, and he was the smartest dog in the world. In fact, he was so smart that most of my friends would say that he understood English. This wasn't simply because he was very obedient and listened to what he was told, although he did do both of those things more often than not. The fact is that Breezy really did understand English.

It was a cool morning and I had just finished delivering my paper route. Breezy usually came with me, running alongside my bike, and this morning was no different. His leash was tied to my handlebars as it always was, and we were cruising along on our way home for some breakfast. Each morning as we passed Mrs. Colby's house, I had to make sure her hundreds of cats weren't loose in the front yard as that always drove Breezy crazy.

In case I forgot to mention it, Breezy got his name because when he found a reason to run, he was gone with the wind just like the breeze. Anyway, we were getting close to Mrs. Colby's house, so I began scanning her garage and front yard. Everything seemed to look clear so I decided it was okay to continue on and Breezy and I kept our pace. It happened so quickly that I never even realized it had happened until it was over.

Breezy had managed to site a couple of Mrs. Colby's cats in the corner of his eye, and that was all she wrote. You see normally if I see Mrs. Colby's cats loose out front, I step off of my bike, get a good grip on Breezy's leash, and we walk on past her house. This way if Breezy decides to try and take off, my two feet are safely planted on the ground and I can manage the situation much better. Well, being that I was still on my bike, when Breezy saw the cats and decided to take off,

he managed to turn my handlebars very abruptly, causing my bike to do a complete end over: flipping over the front tire and making me land on my face and then shoulder.

I didn't notice how bad it was until a minute had passed and my adrenaline had subsided. It was at that point that I knew I was going to need help, but there was no one in sight. You see, my neighborhood is a very country neighborhood with very little traffic. I was hurt quite bad and knew I had only one shot at making it through this situation with minimal effects.

I gave Breezy the command that brought him over to me and in a gentle but firm tone (as I always do when giving Breezy a serious command) told him,

"Go home and get help!"

That was all I had to say and Breezy was gone with the wind. I knew he could make it home without a problem but I was slightly unsure as to just how he would manage to bring help. It must have been almost 45 minutes which is what worried me because I knew Breezy could run home even at a slow pace in under 10 minutes. I began thinking the worst and was sure I would have to attempt to drag myself home on my belly. Just as I had determined to begin the long hard journey home on my belly, I heard a vehicle approaching.

Low and behold, it was my mom in the driver's seat and Breezy riding shotgun.

My mom had barely brought the vehicle to a complete stop when Breezy jumped out the window, ran over to me, and started licking my face as if to say, "Look at me! I did it." My mom ran over with the first aid kit in hand ready to do whatever needed to be done to help me but after closer observation, she realized a trip the emergency room was in order. We had to drive Breezy home as he would never be allowed into the hospital and it was too hot for him to stay in the van.

After dropping Breezy off at home, we turned around and drove to the emergency room. This is when I found out all that Breezy had to go through to get me the help I needed. It turns out that no one was home when Breezy arrived. But he understood the severity of the situation and actually sniffed my mother out. She was next door with her best friend.

My mom said she could hear Breezy barking outside the door and Breezy wouldn't stop for some reason. My mom figured that Breezy was just trying to get a treat or find someone to play with so my mom turned around to walk back into Mrs. Weaver's house. That was when Breezy ran over and took a piece of my mom's pant leg into his mouth and began pulling her towards the van. My mom (being as smart and open minded as she is) didn't hesitate to grab her keys, get into the van and drive the route that she knew I would be on if something had happened. My mom had taught me my paper route, so she knew it well.

It didn't take her but a couple of minutes to find me and another 15 minutes to get me to the hospital after dropping Breezy off. The only thing my mom could say for sure was that Breezy had to have understood what I had told him. She said he wasn't going to quit until he accomplished the task. There is no doubt in my mind that when I told Breezy to go home and get help, he understood every word I said.

[Cherise's note: 'Go home' is a good command to teach your dog. In Los Angeles where I grew up, people just call the dog catcher on strays. However, where I live now in Spokane, on many occasions when a loose dog has come into the park I've heard people tell the dog in a stern voice, "Go home." The dog usually runs off, home I assume. "Go home" seems like a logical thing to tell a stray dog, to me.]

44 BAXTER THE POODLE

Go lie down!

With curly hair that would cover his eyes and a big black nose, Baxter the poodle had a knack for adventure. Constantly getting into trouble by chasing bunnies away from the house, jumping into fish ponds, and eating food out of people's hands, he was a dog with a lot of spirit—and he always wore a smile.

With his five brothers and sisters, he would go on long walks looking for cats to chase and sticks to chew. Baxter was an easygoing standard poodle; he was three feet tall, had white curly long hair, a big belly and a long tail he would wag all the time.

In 2005, Baxter went for a walk to the local dog park with his human sister, Siri. There, he played tag with his friends and chased balls. He had spent around an hour and a half in the park when it was time to go home. On the way home, Siri stopped at a corner store to buy some milk for the house but when she told Baxter to sit outside so she could tie him up, he simply stared at her. After many useless attempts to get the stubborn poodle to sit down, Siri said in frustration,

"Well then, go home!"

At this, the dog perked his ears, turned away from Siri and began to walk away. Out of curiosity, Siri let the five year old dog go and followed him down the street. Baxter didn't notice that Siri was behind him, or if he did, he didn't pay attention. He continued to walk at a happy pace, wagging his tail. The dog then turned the corner onto the street where he lived, stopped outside his front door, and sat down.

Siri stood in amazement. He had walked home all by himself down the busy London streets. The dog looked curiously back at his owner, perhaps wondering where she had come from, and waited for her to promptly open the door and let him inside.

Two weeks later, Baxter went jogging with his human mother, Susan, and was being very slow and then dragging her around to chase squirrels and sniff trees and so he was let off the leash. Baxter didn't like running much. He preferred to slowly make his way down the paths, investigating every tree and rock and looking at everyone who walked by.

Susan continued to jog up the bicycle path for about ten minutes before looping back. Knowing Baxter's habits, she figured he would trot along their normal route at his own pace and she would catch up to him on one of her loops back to check up on him.

As Susan jogged back, she realized Baxter was not on the path that she had left him on. She began to panic. She ran in all directions, fearing the worst, and then for half an hour she ran frantically around the park asking people if they had seen a fluffy white dog wandering around the park, but to no avail. In exasperation, she decided to run to her car where she'd left her phone and call the police in order to get help finding her lost dog.

As she approached the car she noticed something next to it, a big white bag or some shape like it. Upon coming closer to the car she realized it was not a bag at all but her dog. She was amazed. Near as she could surmise, having not seen her when he looked up, he had doubled back and headed to where he knew the car was parked and waited dutifully to go home.

While this is not an example of my dog demonstrating an understanding of English, it does show human-like reasoning, which was astounding.

[Cherise's note: I agree this is astounding. I've known humans with less sense than this demonstrated. The dog remembered they would both need to get in the car in order to go home, so the dog headed for the car in order to make sure he would get home with his human. It does show the ability to reason and not just follow commands, which is all many people think dogs are able to do.]

Baxter also demonstrated comprehension of English phrases when one day he barked when he heard the word 'speak'. When Baxter hears words such as 'cat', 'walk', 'hot dog' or 'treat' he tilts his head to the side and perks his ears up showing an interest in the word. This would only be possible if he were to understand the word. Understanding of the word is shown by a reaction to a word or phrase without being taught through cognitive learning or obedience schools.

When food is placed in his bowl such as pieces of steak and he is asleep in the kitchen or another room, Baxter understands the phrase 'What's this?' He'll investigate his bowl to see if there are in fact any new treats for him to eat. After he receives a treat Baxter will often approach the giver to beg for another, and in the rush of the dinner preparations he gets in the way in the small kitchen.

One day in the bustle of the kitchen, Trevor, his human dad, continually tripped on the dog and in frustration shouted at him,

"Go lie down!"

and looking rather startled, Baxter did just that. He turned and left the kitchen to go lie down in the hallway out of the way. At the end of the meal he was given a treat for being good.

[Cherise's note: We've taught our dogs the command, 'Lie down', but the 'go' part here impresses me. I think most dogs would lie down right there and not understand the 'go' part. I guess the dog could have known from Trevor's tone that he wanted the dog out of the way.]

45 MY CRAZY BASSET HOUND WILEY

*If you eat that, then you could get very
sick and have to visit the vet.*

I have always had a really big appreciation for Basset
Hounds, and over the course of my life I've owned a
few. But none were quite as spontaneous or as much
fun as Wiley. Still, he was quite the trouble maker.

Any time there was food left on the table he would
go after it if no one was around. He certainly did have
quite the nose for knowing when no one was around
so that he could go after a tasty bite of steak or
whatever else might be there for the grabbing. Most
of the time he wouldn't listen to me telling him not to
grab at things, but when it counted most he did
indeed 'drop it'.

[Cherise's note: We have a command for this, 'give'.
When we say, "Give," our dogs drop whatever is in

their mouths: food, toys, each other, trash, what have you. It's a command my sister taught her dogs and one I thought would be really useful, and it is. I suppose those of you with hunting dogs have taught them such a command.]

This was a very good thing both for myself and for Wiley, who might have become very ill had he eaten whatever he happened to grab.

I'm definitely one of those people who is incredibly busy and always on the go, and for this reason I tend to rush through a great many tasks. One of those tasks happens to be cooking, which of course Wiley was always around for no matter what. The smell of grilling meat is something that humans love, but let me tell you dogs love it even more. Wiley was always right there on the back porch with his nose in the air sniffing as if it was the last thing he would ever sniff.

On the particular day in question Wiley had been walked around outside for a good hour before we came inside. Both he and I were enjoying the cool breeze that was coming around to signify the beginning of fall. Wiley seemed to enjoy it just as much as I did since he was running around even more than usual, and he was pushing himself to the limit.

There were a few other people walking their dogs who Wiley said hello to, and I think he really did enjoy just being outside and being able to soak up some pleasant weather. Overall I would have to say that Wiley seemed to be a bit more playful than usual. He was tugging at his leash and really rather forceful about where he wanted to go and what he wanted to do. But in all honesty that has always been part of his charm. He wanted to do things his way and he did not listen to anyone but himself. This allowed him to motivate me at times to leave the house when I knew I should but didn't necessarily want to, because Wiley was right there jumping at his leash.

After we came back home I went ahead and took out the food necessary to cook that night's meal, and it was definitely a meal that Wiley was looking to grab scraps from. I was grilling chicken to make some pita bread sandwiches, and he was right there smelling the food cook. He was amazingly entranced, and I suspected it had to do with the fact that he had been out walking a whole lot. There were a number of times when he brushed up against my leg to let me know that he was incredibly hopeful that I would feed him. I told him,

"If you're a good boy, then I'll give you some of this food as soon as I'm done eating."

At this point I went ahead and grabbed the vegetables and began cooking the sauce for my sandwich, and Wiley seemed to have mysteriously disappeared. Then I turned around and found exactly what he had been up to, which once again was nothing good. Wiley had managed to grab the plastic-wrapped raw chicken breast from the counter, and before I could take it from him he ran into the other room. He was very careful to hop up onto the couch, and then he looked at me wagging his tail with the raw chicken in his mouth. I knew that if he ate raw chicken there was a chance he would become very sick, so I spoke calmly. I told him,

"If you eat that, then you could get very sick and have to visit the vet."

The vet was a place that neither he nor I wanted him to go. His tail continued to wag, and he still wasn't eating it. He was listening to me, so I told him,

"If you drop it, then I'll give you extra scraps."

There have been a whole lot of times when Wiley refused to listen, but this is one time when he did. He dropped the chicken onto the floor. I quickly picked it up and threw it away, got some more out of the fridge, and then proceeded to cook my meal. Wiley sat there the whole time with his tail wagging, and both of us knew that he had indeed been a very good boy and would be rewarded for his good behavior.

It was one of those times when I really felt as if Wiley and I had an understanding and could communicate very well.

With most human beings, I feel as if I'm only partially being heard, but with Wiley I really feel as if he understands what I'm saying. Whether or not he chooses to listen is an entirely different matter, but when it counts the most he usually does. Of course there will always be times when dogs do what they want just like humans do, but I was sure glad this was not one of them. Since then Wiley has not grabbed any chicken from the counter to my knowledge.

46 BLUE THE LITTLE MUTT

See that lady? She's a bad person.
Really bad. She eats doggies.

Growing up I always had a dog or many in my home, and they have all become dear friends to me. When I am feeling sad, angry or excited and if no one is around at the moment I usually just talk to my dog. This seems weird to most people and my mother tells me I'm crazy, but I have had a few moments where my dogs have acted as if they understood exactly what I was saying.

For example, a few years ago I was really mad at my younger brother. I can't remember why. I just remember being so mad that I had to talk to someone about it. No one was around at that moment so I just sat on the couch and my dog Blue came to me and just sat and looked at me. Since he was already there I decided to vent my anger to my little dog. I told him how upset I was at my brother and told him,

"You should be angry at him too since you're my friend and friends have to stick together."

As I finished my rant my brother chose that moment to come back from an errand. As soon as he walked through the door, Blue started barking at him. He and I were both shocked as Blue had never barked at him before. He was wondering why all of a sudden our calm dog decided to bark at him as this was very out of character. He was confused and I was in disbelief.

Blue kept barking at my brother and I led him to his dog house outside and gave him a toy to calm down. When I walked back to the living room my brother wanted to know what had just happened. I told him that I was just ranting about how mad I was at him to Blue and it seemed that Blue was on my side and decided to express his opinion to him. He didn't believe this and merely said,

"Oh yeah, now you think the dog is on your side. Way to be an adult."

He didn't believe me and neither did the rest of my family but I know that my dog understood me. Why else would he uncharacteristically bark at my brother? There was no other reason.

Another moment where my dog seemed to understand me was a few years after that. I found myself yet again having a conversation with my dog. Well not so much a conversation as I was playing with both my niece and Blue.

My niece wanted to play war—I know, kind of a

weird game request from a girl. Blue was one of our soldiers. As our "battle" heated up I ended up "wounded" and lay on the floor. Pretending to be hurt, I extended an arm towards them both and coughing, pleaded for help. When I started to ask for help my dog barked loudly and frantically ran around. Both my niece and I were taken aback as to why my dog started to freak out.

I got up and went to him. As soon as he saw that I was up he stopped barking and came to me. I realized that he thought I was actually hurt and when I asked him for help he tried to give the alert that I was hurt.

What first came to my mind was I was glad that if I was really hurt, then I could count on him to get me help. Secondly I realized that he understood me. I asked for help and he knew exactly what I meant and even tried to help me. I was excited that my niece had witnessed it and could tell my family that Blue did understand what I was saying, as the previous time they hadn't believed me.

Now with a bit more evidence my family started to believe me but it wasn't until last year that they believed me because they actually witnessed Blue responding to me.

We were at a national park and had brought our dog with us so he could enjoy nature as well. We came across a great spot and decided to set up camp there. As we were just sitting around, everyone just engaging in conversation, my cousin made a joke about me. Everyone found it funny and so did I, but I playfully started saying she was mean. I was holding Blue and I pointed at her and told him,

"See that lady? She's a bad person. Really bad. She eats doggies."

He jumped from my lap and barked very angrily at her. Of course my cousin doesn't really eat dogs. Nor is she a bad person. I was just playing around with my dog, but he seemed to think I meant it.

My family was shocked as he is such a gentle dog and rarely barks, and also at the fact that he seemed genuinely upset about what I said. For the entire trip he refused to get near her. Whenever she got close to him he would bark at her.

After this my family also realized that our dog could sometimes understand what we were saying. We all realized that dogs are a lot smarter than we give them credit for.

[Cherise's note: I don't think there's any 'sometimes' about it. I believe that dogs, just like toddler humans, understand everything we say, at least by the tone of our voices, and often by the actual words we say. I don't think dogs are motivated to act on what we say most of the time. Our obedient dog acts when he thinks we expect him to. Our happy-go-lucky dog won't unless he thinks he might get a treat or get petted for acting on it.]

47 OUR BEAGLE SAM

Where's Paul?

Most people would question the sanity of a family owning three beagles, but that is because they never took the time to talk to one, let alone three.

I talk to my beagles all the time. They listen and sometimes respond. The response is in English, but their native heavy British accent and the lack of proper schooling can make it difficult to understand them. However, they have ways to communicate.

Obviously, they understand English. When they need to go outside, we tell them to go by the back door. There are a lot of doors throughout the house, but they go to the back door and politely wait until we get there.

We can call them to come inside, and they usually obey, unless they are chasing a bird or a squirrel. Dogs have priorities in their lives just like humans. Chasing squirrels ranks high on their list.

Life with our two beagles, Hannah and Annie, was pretty peaceful. They slept together. I took the two of them for walks using a special harness for two dogs. However, things changed when a new member entered the picture.

One Saturday we were at a flea market of all places, searching for a book case. Instead, we came home with a third beagle. This yellow and white puppy was to become part of our family over my somewhat mild objections. When we saw the litter of puppies for sale, my wife said, "Can I hold one?"

I remarked, "He's a puppy. All puppies are cute." She agreed. I said, "Remember puppy teeth, house breaking, accidents…" She responded, "He could be my birthday and Christmas present." The events are 19 days apart. I gave up and opened the check book.

Sam is a rascal.

Now seven years old, he is a little less active. As a puppy, he tried to become the alpha dog, and was quickly thwarted in that effort. Sam would nip at Hannah's ears and feet. Hannah will move but never be the aggressor. Therefore, Sam got away with his shenanigans—for a short time. Annie, the cute one, has a strong attachment to Hannah and quickly showed Sam that no one was going to hurt Hannah. Sam learned to watch his step. Annie became his playmate, but Hannah was and is his best dog friend.

As Sam grew, his personality developed. Having never been in a rescue shelter, never forced to scrounge for food and shelter while on the streets or left behind in the woods, his attitude is a little different. He is a good dog but has a real sense of independence. He also has the most hideous bark any dog could ever have. It sounds like a rooster crowing at dawn. Well, nobody is perfect, not even a dog.

Hannah's friendship with Sam has taken on a maternal status. Whenever Sam has to go out into the rain to take care of personal business, he will shake the rain water off and come inside. Hannah will lick his coat dry, and Sammy will sit without moving until she is finished.

However, Sam has his own nurturing qualities which most people do not recognize. Several years ago, my then 22-year-old son, who already had some learning and vision issues, was in a near-fatal car accident. He was in the back seat, and his seat belt was buckled. Someone ran a stop sign. The driver from the car carrying my son swerved to avoid an accident and went into a concrete culvert. The driver was killed. The front-seat passenger has a minor ankle injury,

and my son had to have brain surgery that morning.

When he came to us as a puppy, Sam had only known the good life. However, he earned his place within the family with that incident.

Our son was hospitalized for weeks and in therapy for several more weeks. He had already been legally blind before, and the accident made that worse. When our son came home, Sam stayed by his side. There were some residual effects from the accident, but our son was always in good hands or paws if you prefer.

Sam had already adopted our son before the accident. That bond grew even stronger. Sam sleeps in his room, checks on him and just keeps a close eye on him. We can ask Sam,

"Where's Paul?"

and Sam will go stand by his room or the back door to indicate that he is outside or go to the front door to show us that our son has left with friends.

Perhaps Sam, like our other beagles, Hannah and Annie, cannot speak English. However, there is no question that they understand a lot more than what many people believe. We never told Sam that our son was injured, but he knew something was wrong. He would sit by his bedroom door waiting, while my son was in the hospital.

When we all came home the day the therapy was completed, Sam stayed as close to our son as he could and does so to this day.

They are some who say dogs cannot think. Dogs have emotions. They make themselves a part of your life, if you return the kindness. Can they communicate with you? Of course they can. However, unlike listening to a person while you work on your crossword puzzle, you have to show real attention, just as you would do for a child and like they will do for you, as long as you remember they are more than a dog. They are a part of your family. Sam proved that fact to us.

48 OLIVE THE TOY SHIH TZU

*Olive, I know this is hard, but Jeff is a
part of this family too.*

Owning a toy Shih Tzu has become somewhat of a tradition for the women in my family. My grandma, mom, aunts, sisters, and I each have one of our own. I have had my Shih Tzu, Olive, for nearly six years. I found her shortly after buying my first house. I was concerned about feeling lonely in a new place, so I began checking with local breeders for a house pet. There was a nice older couple outside of town who bred toy Shih Tzu puppies. That is where I spotted her.

Olive was the smallest of her litter, which is really saying something. She was black, except for a brown spot on her head. For some reason, she made me think of olives. The other puppies were constantly knocking her down. I could tell that the owners had a soft spot for her, but I was in love. After several minutes of begging and pleading, I convinced the nice couple to sell her to me. Olive seemed so excited when I brought her back to our new home. I was also pleasantly surprised that it only took a few weeks to potty train her. There was only one problem: I kept losing her. She was so tiny that she could hide just about anywhere. However, as she grew, so did our love for one another.

Olive and I share a very deep and very real connection. She is sweet, mild-mannered, and smart as a whip. She is also very protective of me. Since I work from home, we rarely spend time apart. She has a pillow on my bed and a special spot on the couch. Because she easily fits in my purse, I try to take her with me as often as possible. However, this bond can make it difficult to introduce new people into our lives.

Olive had always been friendly to the guys I dated. It was just a part of her sweet nature. Whenever I had company, she would hop around their ankles and yip for attention. When my husband, Jeff, and I started dating, she seemed especially fond of him. She spent more time cuddled next to Jeff than I did. It wasn't until he proposed that she began to feel threatened.

Suddenly, he was more than a temporary visitor. Jeff was taking over her territory, and she did not like it one bit. She whined when she had to move to a bed on the floor. One day, she took a serious nip at Jeff's finger when he sat too close to her spot on the couch. We tried to be patient, but honestly I felt sorry for her. She only wanted things to go back to the way they were.

The final straw came after Jeff had a particularly bad day at work. I knew he would be in a crabby mood, so I decided to pick up dinner from his favorite restaurant. We arrived back home at the same time. While Jeff went to take a hot shower, I headed into the kitchen to prepare our plates.

I was lifting a large pitcher of water from the refrigerator when Jeff yelled,

"I cannot believe this!"

I was so startled that I nearly dropped the glass pitcher on the floor. I ran towards the bedroom to find out what had happened, but I didn't get very far.

Right there, in the middle of the hallway, was a weird pile of tattered clothes, poop, and wet cotton. Jeff was standing over it, looking as if he would explode, and Olive was directly in front of him.

It took me a second to realize that she had destroyed every piece of clothing he had left on the bedroom floor. She still had a torn sleeve hanging from her mouth.

She did not look afraid at all. In fact, she almost seemed indignant.

It was the most bizarre thing I had ever seen. Jeff wanted to banish her to the deck for the night. I considered it, but instead, I picked her up and carried her into the living room. I brought her to eye-level and softly said,

"Olive, I know this is hard, but Jeff is a part of this family too. This is not okay. Now, go to your bed."

I put her on the floor and watched her trot back down the hall. Jeff looked at me as if I had lost my mind.

"You do know that she doesn't understand a word you're saying, right?" he asked. I just shrugged and went to clean the mess. Later that evening, she quietly crept into the living room while we were watching television.

She sat down in front of Jeff's feet and starting licking his toes.

This quickly melted any hard feelings that he was holding. He rolled his eyes and picked her up. For the rest of the night, she followed him everywhere he went. She even tried to follow him into the bathroom! I know it seems unbelievable, but her entire demeanor changed. It was as if she understood exactly what I had tried to tell her. She was letting him into our little family.

Today, my husband and Olive are close. That rough time is only a distant memory. He loves her almost as much as I do, and I can tell the feeling is mutual. On several occasions, she has suckered him into car rides and trips to the store. I giggle every time I picture this tall, rugged man carrying a toy Shih Tzu around town. His friends give him a hard time, but I think it's the cutest thing ever.

49 DALTON THE TOY POODLE

I love you.

It was September 15th, 2002 when my wife came home from work with a surprise that has changed our lives for the last 11 years. She is a nurse and works in a nursing home with a woman that breeds dogs. As a gift my wife was given a toy poodle. Not a toy poodle, but a "TOY POODLE!" This poodle is coal black and so tiny. It's a pedigreed poodle so we had to fill out paperwork and send his name in to the registry.

Picking Dalton's name was easy, and I'm glad my wife let me do it. I was a big fan of Roadhouse a movie starring Patrick Swayze where he was a cooler. A cooler is a person who throws out anyone starting trouble at a night club. He was very rough and tough and good at his job. When he would first meet people he would say "my name is Dalton." They would say, "Funny, I thought you would be bigger." I had my dog's name, Dalton.

From the very beginning he was amazingly smart. He potty trained immediately. He slept in his special bed. He would know if we had company before we knew.

But what really amazed us was how we would ask him questions or tell him things and he would know what we meant. We would say,

"Dalton, you want to go bye-bye?"

He would run over and stand by the door. We would say,

"Dalton get your blankie."

He would go get his blanket and bring it back for us to cover him with. Our son's name is Donnie. He was only 5 years old when we first got Dalton. We would say,

"Dalton, where's Donnie?"

He would run to the door of the room Donnie was in and bark until we called him back.

I always had cats and dogs as I was growing up. I have had several different breeds of dogs. I heard poodles were very intelligent but after having Dalton I am convinced more than ever. I will tell him to go get his stick and he will play fetch with me for as long as I am willing to throw the stick. I ask him if he is ready for bed and he will run over and lie down in his bed.

Dalton, like the cooler he is named after, does not allow violence. If anyone raises their voice or slaps or pushes someone else, Dalton goes crazy running over barking at them telling them to quit. Even if you are just playing around, don't do it in front of Dalton. He does not allow horseplay.

This peace-keeping mission he's on doesn't just apply to people. We have three other dogs and if they start to rough house with each other he will bark and tell them to knock it off. He doesn't care how big the other dog is. He will always stick up for the little one and stop the big one from hurting it. So we know Dalton understands us in all our everyday conversations and he is in charge of the house.

What really amazed us probably the most is how he acts around babies. We have 8 grandchildren now. When one of the new grandchildren comes over in a car seat or baby basket Dalton will walk over and sit down next to the baby and not move nor allow anyone near the baby. He'll sit for hours keeping people and animals away from the baby. I think if he could hold the bottle he would feed the babies.

I have a doggie door in my back door so my animals can come and go as they please out the back door. The backyard is fenced in so they are safe to run as they wish. I will ask Dalton,

"Is Mommy home?"

He will run outside and see if she has arrived yet. Of course I try to do it at the time she's supposed to be home. If she is home he will race back in and beat her to be waiting at the front door when she enters. He's always so excited to see her when she gets home from work.

We have discussed that Dalton understands English. That is obvious to us. We have known since he was a baby he understood us. But that is by far not the best thing about our precious Dalton.

You see, he not only understands English, he speaks English. So far it's only three little words. But that's more than enough for us. Every time we say to Dalton,

"I love you,"

Dalton always replies, "I love you" in his best poodle voice. You can clearly understand him.

Yes, we have been blessed with wonderful animals our whole lives, my wife and I. Dalton has really brought joy to our family and is considered a little person in our home. We love him so much! He is 11 years old which is like being 77 years old in people years. He is doing great and we look forward to many years with him.

50 MY LADY, A RAT TERRIER

Give me the red ball.

I got a dog when I was growing up named My Lady. She's a rat terrier and highly intelligent. When I was still young, I taught her to climb trees, talk, sing, and tell her colors. She understands everything you say when you speak to her. She sure is a lady. That's why she got that name.

You may be wondering how a dog can talk. Well, she doesn't talk like you and I. She barks her answers or howls when she sings. My favorite is when she says, "I love you." She's such a good dog. I left her with my mom when I left home because Mom loves her way too much to part with her. I make sure that I visit often.

My Lady was a puppy when I got her. Right from the beginning she slept with me. As she grew up, she became very protective of me. I love her very much.

She now sleeps with my Mom. She is so smart that she always knows when I'm coming home to visit. My Mom will tell her to wait by the door for me and that is where I find her when I walk in.

When I was young I used to love to climb this old red bud tree. One day, I was up in the tree and My Lady was under the tree taking a nap. Me being a kid, I thought it would be a good idea to bring her up in the tree with me. So, I climbed down, picked her up and put her on a low branch, then climbed up myself.

I kept putting her higher until I finally got us to my eagles nest. Luckily though, she didn't seem to mind. My Lady curled up and finished her nap. When she woke up, I guess she'd had enough of the tree. She climbed down all by herself. Thus began My Lady's tree climbing adventures.

A few days later, I was up in that tree and My Lady decided to jump up on the lowest branch, then proceeded to the next branch. She kept this up until she had made it to the eagle's nest that I was reading a book in. I was so amazed I couldn't wait to tell my mom. From then on we couldn't keep her out of that tree.

One day I had four balls: red, blue, yellow, and a green one. I had My Lady sitting beside me. I showed her each ball and told her what color it was. I did this a few times every day for a week. So one day I laid them out and told her,

"Give me the red ball."

I was bewildered when she picked up the right ball. "Lucky chance" I thought, so I mixed the balls up and asked her for the green ball. Again she picked up the right ball. I was absolutely amazed.

Not only could she tell her colors, but she understood exactly what I was saying. We played this game for everybody that came over. They were all just as amazed as we were! I decided to teach her other things, too.

She soon learned to understand words like 'mine', 'stay', 'go get', 'I'm sad', 'roll over' and many more. I could set any kind of food on the floor and tell her that it was mine, then leave the room. When I came back the food was untouched. If I would say, "I'm sad," she would crawl up beside me and whimper like she was sad too.

I can ask her a yes or no question, and she will bark once for no and twice for yes.

She has learned so much over the years and has taught me a few things in the process. I have become a Veterinarian Technician because of her, but I still haven't seen a dog as smart as her in the years that I've been working.

When I start singing the songs from cartoons, My Lady will howl along like she's singing. Some sounds actually sound like words. She says "I love you" in her own way, but if you listen real close, you can understand her perfectly.

I say she is a lady because she never ever potties in the house, never speaks out of turn, and never gulps down her food. She has been this way since she was first brought into our home. She is always sweet to small children and adults alike.

My Lady will paw at the air when she knows it is time to eat. If she is told,

"It's not time yet,"

then she will go lie down on her bed until she is called for supper. She never barks at strangers unless they try to touch me or she suspects they are a bad person.

I loved teaching her new things. I don't do much teaching anymore because I feel she has learned enough. Besides I'm not always around long enough to reinforce the new lessons. I like to think of it as her graduating.

When she is old enough, I will get a Rat Terrier for my own daughter to love and teach. It will help them both grow up smart and form a bond that no one can break. After all, dogs are people too.

CONCLUSION

In 2004, a Border Collie named Rico convinced the scientific community that dogs can figure out the meanings of English words the first time they hear the words. When the scientists met Rico, he already knew how to play fetch with 200 different toys his humans had named for him.

The scientists played fetch with Rico for a few months, and they introduced new toys he hadn't ever seen before. To rule out body language as a way the dog's humans were telling Rico which toy to get, the scientists put the toys in another room where the dog couldn't see his humans while he was choosing which toy to retrieve. To make it even more complicated, they put the new toy in the other room along with several familiar toys.

Seven out of each ten times with many different new toys, Rico brought the new toy when they asked for it by name. He figured out the name of the new toy by the process of eliminating all the other possibilities! The process of elimination is a higher thinking ability than just remembering from being taught something.

It gets even better. They didn't show Rico the new toy after that, and they didn't talk about it. Four weeks later, they played fetch with Rico and the new toys again. Half the time, Rico still remembered the name of each new toy and correctly fetched it. In the published literature of the study, they say this is about how often three-year-old human toddlers are able to do the same thing.

Word Learning in a Domestic Dog:
Evidence for "Fast Mapping"
Juliane Kaminski, Josep Call, and Julia Fischer
Science 11 June 2004
Vol. 304 no. 5677 pp. 1682-1683
DOI: 10.1126/science.1097859
http://www.sciencemag.org/content/304/5677/168
2.full

Most of the other research I read about dogs and humans communicating emphasized our pets' ability to read our body language. For example, the staff at Duke University's Evolutionary Anthropology Department claim that dogs are better at reading human body language than chimpanzees are.
http://evolutionaryanthropology.duke.edu/research/dogs/research/understanding-communicative-intentions

Some of the dogs in this book really did figure out what a word meant the first time they heard it. Others read human body language or tone. All loved their humans and wanted to please them.

ABOUT THE AUTHOR

Cherise Kelley writes the Dog Aliens novels, inspired by her own dogs, Raffle and Oreo, who she and her husband rescued from the animal shelter.

Dog Aliens 1: Raffle's Name is based on the true story of adopting and naming Raffle, a Queensland Heeler / German Shepherd mix. The fictional part is that Raffle's true name is Clem, and that he is from the planet Kax, and he has mind control abilities.

Dog Aliens 2: Oreo is based on the true story of adopting Oreo and seeing him give his adopted 'brother' Raffle the hardest time ever, before they finally got along. The fictional part is that Raffle keeps trying to tell Oreo they are both aliens from the planet Kax, and Oreo thinks Raffle is nuts!

Both books are available wherever you buy paperbacks or ebooks online. More books are planned in the series.

DOG ALIENS 1: RAFFLE'S NAME
CHAPTER 1: CAR TRIP

Wow, my parents' human was taking me somewhere in the car alone, just the two of us! This was the first time that had ever happened. I had been in the car before, to go to the dog park or to the vet, but Mom and Dad had always been along, and my brothers and sisters, before other humans had adopted them.

This was going to be a long car trip. I could tell because I smelled food in the bag he had thrown into the back seat. Maybe he would drive us to the woods and then take me for a long walk, and we would explore a wilderness area together! This was odd so late in the day, but hey, if we spent enough time alone together having fun, we might finally bond. I would like that. At least, I thought I would like that.

My previous life memories about the dog bond were a bit hazy. I could remember everything I ever knew about mining jex. I could remember several hundred commands that humans had taught me, in my previous lives. I knew that humans could bond with Kaxians (and with Niques, but who cared about them?). Everyone said the dog bond was lovely, something to strive for. I thought probably I had bonded with humans before, but I honestly could not remember for sure, and I could not remember what it was like. I thought it would be nice, though.

I looked over at this human who had bonded with my parents, to try and catch some body language that told me what he was thinking, where we were going, or anything interesting at all.

He didn't look at me, not even a glance ever, for the two hours we were in the car together.

I thought this was strange, but I made excuses for him. This was my first time riding in the front seat, and he was driving, after all. "Maybe he finds driving too engrossing a task and can't take his attention away from driving to look at me. Yeah, that's probably it," I told myself.

He switched on the radio and sang along with some nonsensical songs, hitting the steering wheel to the beat of the music and pretty much ignoring me. He answered his phone and chatted about his job with a female. He looked out the window as the sun set, whistling a tune.

I told myself, "Just be content that he took you along," and I did my best to look like I was having fun. I looked out the window, too, and watched the desert go by.

After ninety minutes or so, he turned, and we were going up a mountain road. My parents' human did drive up into the woods! It seems a long way to any woods, from the deserts of Southern California, but there are huge pine trees a few hours' drive away, up any of the local mountains.

It was dark when he stopped the car and set the parking brake, which again, I thought was odd. Humans don't see well in the dark. He put on a coat, put the small bag of food on his back, let me out, and called me to follow him over to where a trail headed off into the woods. How nice! We were going for a walk together!

I ran to him quickly, wagging my tail to show him how happy I was to be singled out and taken for a walk, all on our own. I wasn't even on a leash!

It was a lovely walk in the woods, even if it was a bit short. We went up a little hill. There were many different types of insects in the nearby bushes, chirping at us. I could smell lizards, snakes, squirrels, and gophers. There were no other humans around, which I figured was why I wasn't on a leash. The puppy that I was (and perhaps the wolf part of me) wanted to chase after a squirrel that ran across the trail. Memories from previous lives told me the human wanted me to stay by his left heel, though, so I did.

My parents' human sighed then. This confused me. I was 99% sure he wanted me to walk by his left heel and not chase the squirrel. I was doing what he wanted, so why was he unhappy?

CPSIA information can be obtained at www.ICGtesting.com
Printed in the USA
LVOW07s0835121215

466395LV00004BB/356/P

9 781494 263805